HOW TO WIN WITH WILLPOWER

HOW TO WIN WITH

75 Strategies to Increase Self-Discipline, Motivation, and Success

ALIYA LEVINSON, LMSW, MA, CPC, ELI-MP

ROCKRIDGE
PRESS

For general information on our other products and services or to obtain technical support, please contact our Customer Care Department within the United States at (866) 744-2665, or outside the United States at (510) 253-0500.

Rockridge Press publishes its books in a variety of electronic and print formats. Some content that appears in print may not be available in electronic books, and vice versa.

TRADEMARKS: Rockridge Press and the Rockridge Press logo are trademarks or registered trademarks of Callisto Media Inc. and/or its affiliates, in the United States and other countries, and may not be used without written permission. All other trademarks are the property of their respective owners. Rockridge Press is not associated with any product or vendor mentioned in this book.

Interior and Cover Designer: Sean Doyle
Art Producer: Janice Ackerman
Editor: John Makowski
Production Editor: Nora Milman
Cover Photograph: © chuckcollier/istock
Author photo courtesy © Ian Deveau

ISBN: Print 978-1-64611-327-9 | eBook 978-1-64611-328-6
R0

To my
12-year-old self—we did it!
And to my mother, Cara Levinson, for
all of her support on this book.

Contents

Resources   154

References   155

Index   166

Introduction

Well, you officially did it. You went out and bought a book on willpower—or maybe you simply picked it up and are currently skimming through the pages at the bookstore. Either way, something drew you to this book, and you followed that "something" and now it's literally in your hands.

Go you.

I know. You may be thinking, "I haven't really *done* anything yet. I simply picked up a book. Is that really cause for celebration?"

Let me tell you, your mere interest in exploring the possibility of increasing your willpower means something.

It means that this subject stirred something inside of you. Your mind is open to the possibilities. You're interested in learning more. And best of all, there's a part of you that knows, deep down, that you're capable of creating positive change.

Imagine being able to tap into willpower easily and more often. Imagine "exerting willpower" being less of a to-do and more, well, habitual. What might that mean for you in the long run? What might life look like if you could finally establish a healthier lifestyle, kicking that specific habit and committing to better ones? Maybe your goals are career oriented. Perhaps you want to shift a few priorities—or maybe you want to transform your entire life.

Now, if you're anything like me, maybe up until this point you've had a bumpy relationship with the word *willpower*. When I used to think of the word *willpower*, I imagined the Michael Jordans of the world who somehow just *do*. I pictured friends and colleagues who seemed to have this innate ability to consistently rise and successfully take on all personal and professional challenges.

For the longest time, I did not view myself as that sort of person. I was much more comfortable with the things that somehow landed in my lap, as opposed to the ones I had to go out and get. I found myself saying yes to low-hanging fruit (jobs and opportunities) as opposed to challenging myself to reach higher, get out there, and try for things that might speak more to my deeper passions. Early on in my career, I took a job in real estate that was to some extent "handed" to me. Although I was appreciative of the position, I was hardly passionate about the work. I thought about looking for something that more accurately reflected my interests: writing, psychology, something artistic even. But I ultimately settled on this opportunity because it was "right there" and seemingly steady. Even after finally deciding to go for my master's in social work, I found myself in the same position post grad school: taking social work jobs that, while closer to my area of interest, still felt less creative and less challenging—and they didn't exactly spark my passion. Perhaps I didn't want to put myself to the test of actually thriving in a job well matched to my skills, or perhaps I questioned my ability to succeed.

Either way, sitting pretty in jobs that were comfortable became quite uncomfortable. I grew tired of not giving my all and feeling like I was settling. I realized I *did* want to see myself thrive, and deep down I knew I could.

Then I learned about the field of coaching, and instantly everything clicked: This is what I was missing. This way of thinking, of teaching, of helping, of living. This is where I wanted to give my all. But would I actually be able to build a successful coaching business? Bring in a steady stream of clients? Turn nothing (a non-existent coaching practice) into something: a meaningful and productive enterprise? To be honest, I didn't have the answers to these questions. But I realized that building a successful coaching business would present me with the opportunity I wanted most: to strengthen my own willpower while helping others like me do the same.

That's when my journey really began and became exciting. I've worked with many clients on creating results they previously doubted they could create—from building their own coaching practices to achieving freedom, connection, and fulfilment in their personal and professional lives—and consequently, they've come to understand how doubt and frustration are just normal feelings that have no bearing on their capacity to achieve.

And now, I'm so excited to share these 75 proven strategies with *you*! Whatever willpower challenge you're facing—whether it's thriving in the face of temptation or forgoing negative self-talk—I have many research-based strategies to help support and guide you. If you're ready to finally overcome obstacles and achieve those personal and professional goals, you're in the exact right place.

I'm here as your partner, cheerleader, and coach. Let's take this journey together. Yes, you can!

Chapter One

Willpower 101

When we think of the word *willpower*, dozens of different meanings come to mind. When I spent time brainstorming my own definition of willpower, I finally settled on this: "Willpower is the ability to endure in the face of a challenge." But when I asked my husband how he would describe willpower, he said that willpower is "resisting temptation" and "sticking to a goal." This made me realize that your definition may be similar or entirely different.

So, what really *is* willpower, anyway?

And on top of that, is it something we *can* actually acquire?

In the past, I couldn't help but view willpower like some family heirloom that's passed down from generation to generation—where the individuals lucky enough to be in that family were the ones lucky enough to inherit this elusive trait.

But is it a trait? Or is willpower something that can be learned and strengthened through practice and conscious effort?

Is *willpower* achieved through *willpower*?

In this chapter, we're going to learn the answers to these questions, as well as the fascinating reasons why willpower matters to you, me, and all of us.

What Is Willpower?

According to the *Merriam-Webster Dictionary*, the definition of willpower is—drumroll please—"energetic determination."

I don't know about you, but for me, this definition is relieving. It means that *willpower* and feeling energized, positive, and—dare I say it—excited go hand in hand.

So, overexertion? Toiling away? Those aren't necessarily prerequisites for successfully progressing toward your goal.

According to our good friend *Merriam-Webster*, it's all about embodying a sort of "lively fortitude," which is actually quite the opposite of overexertion.

Point 1 willpower!

Now let's talk business. Or rather, history. Because in order to fully grasp the concept of willpower, we first need to learn about the key figures whose research led to our current understanding of the way willpower works.

Back in the 1960s, a pioneering research psychologist in personality theory named Walter Mischel and his colleagues conducted the "marshmallow experiment." In a nutshell, the work examined the foundation of delayed versus instant gratification. In the experiment, preschoolers were given a choice of consuming a treat, such as a marshmallow, immediately or holding out for a larger treat 10 minutes later. Follow-up studies years later found that the youngsters who had opted for the larger delayed treat were more likely to achieve higher test scores, exhibited greater social and cognitive competence, and experienced other positive outcomes later in life. The children who chose that initial marshmallow were more likely to exhibit difficulty with self-control into adulthood than the ones who opted for the delayed gratification, who generally continued to display a strong ability to self-regulate.

So, if you give a mouse a cookie, and he doesn't hold out for a better treat, is he destined for a lifelong struggle with willpower?

Not necessarily, according to Roy Baumeister, PhD. In his now-famous study from the mid-1990s, Baumeister and several colleagues placed a group of college students in a room with two plates of food—on one, radishes, and on the other, freshly baked cookies. Half of the students were instructed to enjoy the cookies, while the other half were told to resist and only eat the radishes.

After they ate, each group had to complete a puzzle that was, unbeknownst to them, unsolvable. The group that was required to resist the cookies (that is, to exert willpower) gave up on solving the puzzle faster than the group that was allowed to indulge in them.

These results helped inform Baumeister's theory of "ego depletion," a once widely accepted concept that mental resources become depleted after activity that tests our willpower.

So, should we go reschedule our days so we don't run out of energy for our high-priority tasks?

And, is it possible for us to strengthen our willpower in adulthood even if it wasn't as strong in our childhood? Let's explore.

Can My Willpower Be Increased?

First, we need to understand what optimal willpower requires.

Studies suggest that to exercise willpower, we must have sufficient levels of glucose, the sugar in our blood that provides us with energy. In other words, having enough willpower depends on having enough energy. Without adequate blood glucose, we likely won't have the willpower to manage our emotions, focus our attention, monitor social behaviors, and resist cravings with relative ease.

So! According to these studies on glucose and what we learned from Baumeister, it seems like we all have a finite, or limited, reserve of willpower, no matter who we are.

But what if the *theories* are finite, not the *willpower*? Stay with me . . .

Carol Dweck, PhD, author of *Mindset* and a leading researcher in the field of motivation, posits that the people who tend to believe that willpower is a limited resource, which must be replenished, *act* that way. On the other hand, the people who believe willpower is plentiful and isn't easily used up act *that way*.

Hold up. Is Dweck suggesting we simply need to *believe* in order to achieve our goals?

As her research demonstrates, when it comes to the elusive recipe of willpower, believing in the bounty of willpower (and simply *believing* on its own account) is one of several important ingredients.

One of my coaching clients—we'll call her Maggie—was finally at the top of her game in her business. We started working together, and within six months, she had more than doubled her income, had negotiated a higher salary, and was now regularly closing high-stakes deals. When Maggie began believing in her own ability to create more impact and income in her career, more often than not, she did!

So, with the belief part down pat, what other elements are needed to increase willpower?

For Maggie, it was learning to identify and prioritize what mattered most to her, as opposed to engaging in tasks to appease others.

According to research psychologist Mark Muraven, exerting self-control for autonomous reasons—or being internally compelled out of your own volition—requires less effort than doing it to please people.

To illustrate, when Maggie separated the social and business opportunities that mattered most to her from the ones she was simply attending for the sake of others, she found she was able to sustain her efforts for longer and with greater engagement.

The only thing that differentiates Maggie from you and me is that she's implemented this process. If Maggie can strengthen her willpower, we can, too! Let's find out how by looking at how the brain works with regard to these kinds of decisions—and how it all got started.

Where Does Willpower Come From?

You're at the movies, and although you're tempted to purchase Raisinets, you opt for the apple in your pocket instead. Great choice! You peel yourself off your oh-so-comfortable sofa to attend your fitness class rather than pressing "next episode" on that Netflix series. Nice work! Choices like these are primarily made in your prefrontal cortex, the part of your brain that's responsible for decision-making. These are your brain's executive functions at play, the mind's way of saying "Resist temptation!" "Plan ahead!" and "Let's make a different choice, even if it feels like a challenge in the moment!" Isn't it nice to know that our brain is actually designed to help us succeed?

And not just succeed but *survive*. In her book *The Willpower Instinct*, health psychologist Kelly McGonigal explains how way back in the day—I'm talking hundreds of thousands of years ago—early *Homo sapiens* had many a mystery to solve: *How do I attain adequate shelter? Find a mate? Discover edible foods? All without being eaten myself!*

And these weren't our only responsibilities. If we somehow successfully caught dinner, found a mate we vibed with, built our dream cave, and thwarted the lion who was chasing us, we still had one quite pressing responsibility that some 100,000 years ago we finally wised up to: We had to make friends.

Wouldn't you know it? Being part of a group or tribe helped us get our individual needs met. And as in any functioning social group, in order to maintain our coveted position in the crew, we had to play by its rules: making sure we contributed, treated others cooperatively, and didn't steal anyone's food. Or mate for that matter.

Enter willpower, that "energetic determination" we humans were endowed with that helps us abide by a group's ethos. Willpower enabled early men and women to exhibit control, regulate emotions, and cope with stress—all so they could work and play with others, remain part of the tribe, and ultimately survive.

Why Is Willpower Important?

A client of mine, let's call him Bob, sought out my coaching services because he wanted support making a career transition. Although his current job was in his area of expertise, it was wearing on him. He felt undervalued, underpaid, and overworked. On top of his discontent with his career, a year earlier, his long-term relationship had ended. Bob wanted a shift in his professional and personal life but felt overwhelmed by the idea of change.

When we first began working together, it was clear that sending out résumés wasn't on the docket for Bob just yet. Besides not yet knowing which career path to explore, the idea of researching and applying to jobs after a full day's work felt too heavy a task.

The American Psychological Association defines willpower as "the ability to resist short-term temptations in order to meet long-term goals." Bob had assumed that successfully moving forward meant replacing video games with writing cover letters and giving up watching late-night movies.

But when we examined Bob's circumstances and thoughts, we uncovered the real habit that needed changing. Bob had a deep-seated belief that he couldn't move himself forward toward his goals. He was stuck in a pattern of habitual thinking. Instead of being the driver of his own life, he felt like a mere passenger along for the ride.

Through coaching, Bob realized he didn't necessarily have to make all new friends or even switch jobs to feel better. He simply needed to challenge his thoughts around not believing he could.

American industrialist Henry Ford famously said, "Whether you think you can or think you can't, you're right."

When Bob began noticing his knee-jerk "I can't do this" thoughts, he began planning for and responding to them, instead of immediately quitting.

This simple positive shift triggered tons of forward momentum for Bob. He began organizing events for his group of friends. Saying no to activities he'd formerly begrudgingly agree to. Making and achieving daily action plans. And he hit his personal goal of rewriting his résumé and landing interviews months ahead of schedule.

Along with all this, Bob experienced a number of other unexpected transformations, including increased confidence, greater emotional fortitude, and finally saying goodbye to formerly "impossible to break" habits.

Bob accomplished these things through energetic determination, not through pain or suffering. In fact, he told me he'd hoped for change but couldn't believe how quickly it happened. He previously felt a weight lifted each time he left our sessions, but now he says, "It's like the weight isn't even there."

Chapter Two

Building a Willpower Habit

All right! So far, you've learned about the marshmallow experiment, the impact of glucose on willpower, the importance of believing in an expansive reserve of willpower, and good ol' Bob and the way he enacted positive change in his life.

You, my friend, have officially passed Willpower 101. #ConfettiToss!

Maybe you're wondering what it takes to get to the next level. Or you have, like so many of us, a more profound question: Should I expect this to actually work for *me*?

Fear not! If you've wondered about this yourself, or experienced even slight doubt about your ability to succeed, consider yourself ahead of the game. The act of simply recognizing your own doubt is, as it so happens, a critical first step to building your willpower habit. Why? Well, when we identify our own doubts, we can then anticipate them, plan around them, and learn to overcome them.

More on how later in this chapter.

In fact, in addition to polishing our personal doubt-detector skills, we'll be learning how to set a clear goal, make it easy to navigate through obstacles, and put a prevention plan in place—so whether you take two steps forward or two steps back, you'll be fully covered.

Get Motivated

Remember Carol Dweck from chapter 1? Well, in addition to her thoughts on willpower reserves, she also explains that people tend to operate with either a fixed mindset or a growth mindset.

When you operate from a fixed mindset, you believe your personality traits, talents, and skills are set and—for the most part—won't change. Your abilities are your abilities, and in this mindset, your typical mentality is "I'm either good at this or I'm not, and if I'm not good at it, well, there's no point in trying, because I likely can't succeed."

A growth mindset, on the other hand, encourages—wouldn't you know it—growth! These folks find it riveting to encounter a challenge, as it's an opportunity to grow, stretch, learn, acquire new skills, and become more capable. When you're operating within a growth mindset, you believe in your ability to transform.

Now, perhaps you're reading this and thinking, "Fixed mindset sounds a lot like me." Totally cool. I've experienced a fixed mindset for most of my life. Only today, I want to invite you to draw a line in the sand with me.

Right here. Right now. Let's choose to believe that positive, lasting change is inevitable if we want it to be.

In fact, Carol Dweck has found that simply *knowing* about these two mindsets can support us in thinking and operating in growth-oriented ways. Now that we know it, let's try on our growth-mindset hat.

From here on out, we're going to view achieving and growing as an inevitability that will occur while we're endeavoring to reach our goal.

Might we get discouraged at times? Sure! Might we get tired? Maybe.

But we're not going to make those things mean *anything* about our ability to succeed. We've learned that they are a natural part of the process.

And! When we're wearing our growth-mindset hat, we know that encountering certain challenges that *could* stop us doesn't actually mean we *should* stop. Instead of getting discouraged, we're going to get curious and discerning. We're going to find the opportunity in the obstacle and appreciate the challenge for what it is: a way to help us grow.

Feel me? Good. Because I'm going to be right here with you, sharing 75 powerful strategies for how to do just that.

Set One Clear Goal

All right, my friend. Let's talk goals! Specifically, *your* goals. I have a hunch you didn't pick up this book by accident. Maybe you saw the word *willpower* and thought, "I could use some of that." Maybe you're eager to build more intrinsic motivation or break a certain long-time habit.

Whether or not you've tried accomplishing this goal before, let's wipe the slate clean. Okay? Right now. This moment. Today!

You're in a perfect position to begin this process in a way that's powerful, authentic to you, and most importantly, gets you where you want to go. So, where *do* you want to go? Let's start here: What drew you to this book? What's driving your desire to increase your willpower? Remember, there's absolutely no right or wrong answer. No one else needs to know except you, me, and these pages.

Spend some time brainstorming, then go ahead and write your reason here (or on a separate piece of paper):

_____

_____

_____

Great work. Now that we understand why strengthening your willpower is important, let's take it a step further. Picture that you've followed the strategies laid out in this book and have successfully made it to the end and achieved your goal.

Tell me, what did you accomplish? Did you stop biting your nails? Have you incorporated fruits and veggies into your diet? Are you spending more time with your kids? Are you now exceeding your sales goals? What, specifically, did you achieve? Take the time you need to brainstorm and get clear on the results you desire most. What incredible goal do you have for yourself?

When you're ready, write down your goal on the following lines (or on a separate piece of paper) in the past tense. Yep! As if *you've already achieved it*. In other words: "I no longer bite my nails!" or "I quit smoking!"

_____

_____

_____

Your brain believes the information you feed it, and it can't *exactly* separate when you've fed it fiction and fantasy versus reality. (More on that later.) So, when you visualize yourself already having achieved your goal, your brain will start to operate from that place, too. How's that for a *head* start?

Also, as you go through the strategies in this book, any time you get stuck, come back here and reground yourself in the feeling of achieving your goal, as if you already have!

Steer Clear of Temptations

Here's the thing. We *all* encounter distractions. Yet, many are actually *perceived distractions*, our mind's attempt at redirecting us toward "easier" tasks. Ones we're familiar with. Proficient at.

Case in point: While writing this book I *just so happened* to recall various obligations I *had* to tend to. I'd open my laptop but would suddenly notice the dishes that, well, weren't going to wash themselves. Or I would check social media for just a minute and see my BFF from elementary school! Who I haven't spoken to in decades! We should definitely reconnect—today! Imagine leaving her hanging another 12+ years?!

My excuses and disruptions came in a very convincing package. They likely will for you, too. You will find a seemingly valid, logical reason for why now is the perfect time to attend that weekly work happy hour you've never been to since being hired, instead of cleaning your apartment.

Our mind is like a multilane highway. Nerve impulses drive down the same neural pathways repeatedly, and those pathways become reinforced. So, when you ask your brain to take a new route, it's understandable that resistance appears. Now that we know this, when excuses arise and our urge is to go the same direction we've always gone, we can instead pause and recognize this inclination.

And then we can step back and appreciate, even honor, our mind for trying its darndest to keep us on that old faithful road, before we instead say, "Wait! In order to get something I've never gotten, I need to do something I've never done."

And as comfortable as it may feel to take that same tried-and-true path, I'm actively choosing to turn left instead of right. Keep going instead of stopping. Recognize those distractions for what they are: a long-lost friend whose happiness doesn't depend on my call or a happy hour I can miss.

So, what obstacles might appear suddenly and unexpectedly for you? What sneaky thoughts may try pulling you off course and convince you it's better to chill and watch Netflix than hit the track and run? A few of my faves are:

Everyone else is doing it.

I need the sleep anyway.

One little bite can't hurt.

My dog deserves a nice long walk.

They can all feel like, and may even be, truths. For example, you may really have to walk your dog, but if this is the third walk within the hour and you have a project that needs finishing, you may want to ask yourself how necessary that additional walk is. When these distractions or excuses come up, we want to be aware of them so we can label them as a distraction as opposed to a new direction for our day.

Write your top five distractions here (or on a separate piece of paper):

_____

_____

_____

_____

_____

Set a Plan in Place

Now we know that obstacles and temptations are a normal part of this willpower process. So, how do we avoid them?

The answer? *We don't.*

Instead we *plan* for them. Yep!

Being cognizant of the sort of sneaky distractions we might be prone to gives us a kind of competitive advantage. Now, instead of letting our neighbor's last-minute request for a babysitter or that enticing plate of cookies pull us off course, we can anticipate and prepare for how we'll respond when these or similar unexpected obstacles crop up.

So! When one of your top five distractions appears—or you find yourself creating a totally sound argument on why it's okay to sleep in *"just this once"*—how will you remember to silence that siren call? To ignore the bait? Take a moment or two to brainstorm how you will respond to sneaky obstacles.

Here are three ideas to consider to help you stay the course:

1. **Plan ahead.** In order to stick to a plan, we need to have one in the first place. If, for example, your goal is to quit smoking and you're attending a baseball game on Saturday, consider what alternate activity you might engage in during that fifth inning when you might typically choose to take a smoke break outside the stadium.

2. **Work the plan beforehand!** Spend time picturing how you'll respond when asked to "join the gals" for a cigarette. Anticipate those feelings that might come up. A craving? Jealousy toward other smokers? Put a preventive measure in place: "When Jenny asks me to smoke a cigarette, I'm going to say 'no thanks,' and I'll chew a stick of gum instead and focus on the tingly sweet taste of the cinnamon while rooting for my team." By having an alternate plan on standby, you create another option for yourself besides joining the group and passing the lighter.

3. **Give up black-and-white thinking.** If you happen to slip up, there's no need to throw in the towel or consider yourself not cut out for this. Slipping up gives us an amazing opportunity to learn from what didn't go as planned, gain insight into what we'll do differently next time, and course correct!

Now it's your turn. Using the following lines (or on a separate piece of paper), write a personal prevention plan. To work, your plan should feel natural, doable, and authentic to you. You've got this!

_____

_____

_____

_____

_____

_____

Chapter Three

Your Personalized Willpower Program

Consider this book your friendly companion on your journey to strengthening your willpower. You're about to receive access to many different options for building your willpower habit, and they aren't one-size-fits-all. So! You most certainly don't need to implement the ones that don't feel like a good fit for you. But when you lean into the ones that *do*, they will prove incredibly powerful.

Also, although each strategy packs a powerful punch on its own, take it from Aristotle, who said, "The whole is greater than the sum of its parts." When you use these strategies in conjunction with one another, you'll be prepping yourself for the total willpower package. Think of it like a well-balanced meal: You can just eat the apple or the sweet potato or the fish, but when you eat them all together, it's a well-balanced diet, providing the energy you need to be healthy and succeed.

Determine Your Time Frame

Now that you've set your goal, let's come up with a solid, feasible time frame so you stay on track. And no need to worry. Having a time frame doesn't mean you're going to have to turn into a regimented robot to accomplish what you want. In fact, it's quite the opposite. Implementing a time frame means that, together, we'll be moving the needle forward little by little so we can get you where you want to be by the time you want to be there.

Now, in the past I myself felt restricted by adhering to a specific time frame—as if scheduling myself would somehow limit my freedom. What I came to realize was that having a time frame and organizing the where, when, and how of the process actually alleviates indecision and speculation. Instead of wondering "Will I really do it?" we can embrace the freedom that comes with getting a solid plan on paper and then not having to worry about it. The result: no more being constrained by some wishy-washy idea of how you'll get things done that keeps you in limbo as opposed to in motion.

So, how do we decide on a time frame that best suits us? What's the best method for setting goals in a way that's realistic yet still motivating?

By setting goals the smart way—literally!

SMART goals are a way to set goals that meet specific criteria:

S: Specific. What do I want to achieve? (Example: I want to save $2,600 for a vacation.)

M: Measurable. How will I measure achieving this goal? (I will set aside $100 each week for 26 weeks. I will keep this money in a separate account.)

A: Attainable. Is this goal challenging but still possible? (Yes, my basic living expenses (rent, food, transportation, and the like) are still met if I save $100 per week.)

R: Realistic. Can I realistically achieve this goal? (Yes. I can save $50 a week by bringing my lunch to work, and another $50 or more by avoiding the mall.)

T: Time Bound. When do I want to accomplish this goal by? (I want to reach my goal in 26 weeks.)

Now that you've learned how to "think SMART," it's your turn. On the lines provided (or on a separate piece of paper), create your smart goal plan. You can write a six-month, one-month, and one-week SMART goal plan, or whatever works for you!

_____

_____

_____

_____

_____

_____

Set Your Course

All right, friend! Let's make all this even more tangible for you, and you specifically.

Flip to page vii, skim through the table of contents, and tell me: Which strategies are you *most* drawn to? What feels intriguing and doable? Which strategies feel like an outright no?

There's no absolute *correct* answer except what feels right to you. Because this book is hardly one-size-fits-all. In fact, let's think of this as more of a choose-your-own-adventure book! Just by reading through them, you'll have a sense of which strategies might be easiest or most exciting to apply. Find a strategy you vibe with? You can use that strategy five days in a row or 75 days in a row if you'd like. Heck, you can implement strategy #43 for three days consecutively, and strategy #21 every other day for a week. There's no right or wrong when it comes to applying these strategies, as long as we stay in that forward momentum and, simply put, *keep applying them.*

So! Using the following table, go ahead and write out your strategy schedule. If your strategies extend beyond the scope of the chart, feel free to use a big ol' sheet of poster board and hang it in your office, type your strategies into an Excel spreadsheet, jot them in your planner, or map them out on your whiteboard if you have one. Just get them down somewhere you'll be sure to see them.

Day	Strategy	Page Number
1		
2		
3		
4		
5		
6		
7		

Stick with It!

You've done it! You've made it to the end of chapter 3. Now it's time to dive into 75 mighty cool strategies. Go ahead and give yourself a wink in the mirror or pat on the back. If you find that awkward, silly, or even undeserved, then consider it your very first challenge. Failing to celebrate even what may seem like minor progress is the reason most of us fail to keep going. By recognizing the seemingly small steps, we're helping ourselves stay positive and proud—two emotions we want to embrace. By making it here, you've taken a significant stride forward and are doing something many others only dream about. It's easy to simply wish for good things, but you're primed to actually make them happen.

Now, before we begin, let's remember the importance of three concepts: focusing on momentum, staying consistent, and challenging yourself to put in the effort each day. You have an incredible opportunity in front of you that you've said yes to, which is exciting—you're journeying toward a goal that you set for yourself! And don't forget: Although we're focused on moving the ball forward, if you miss a day or two, there's no need to fret. Just get back on the horse and remember I'll be right here waiting for you.

Chapter Four

The Strategies

#1 Reframe Obstacles

WHY IT WORKS

Have you ever noticed the tendency we humans have to label things? Good, bad, right, wrong, easy, hard? Our brain does this in an effort to organize and categorize and, ultimately, simplify life for us. If we know something's good, we can move toward it. Bad—away from it.

However! When we label things as positive or negative, we change the way we approach and interact with those things. For example, if we view that 6:00 a.m. fitness class as something that will prove difficult, we'll likely dread attending it. But if we see it as an opportunity for me-time, to watch the sunrise on our way there? We'll become inspired by it!

Consider this: When we label or have an encouraging or discouraging thought, we're simultaneously placing a bet on that thought and rooting for it to win. Think, "I'll take 'Dread the Gym' for 500, please!" So why not bet on the thoughts that will help us progress, and re-label experiences that will move us forward as positive? For example, instead of labeling snacking on veggies instead of carbs as restrictive or impossible, give it a positive spin and begin substantiating that new, more encouraging reframe.

HOW TO DO IT

1. **Let go of unsupportive labels.** Gently acknowledge the way you're thinking or speaking about a certain task: "It's too hard" or "I'm not cut out for this."

2. **Build a case for it.** "Even though it feels hard in this moment, I know getting up and attending this gym class will help me jumpstart my day."

3. **Foster your new thought.** Think it, write it, read it, repeat it!

#2 Take Advice from Your Future Self

WHY IT WORKS

Want to hear something fascinating? Studies show that we often treat our future self like an *entirely different person*! This means when we picture ourselves five, 10, or 20 years in the future, we feel disconnected—kind of like that far-out version of ourselves is a stranger. Knowing this helps shed light on why our long-term goals don't always feel urgent. In the present, it doesn't click that the person benefitting from our future planning is, in fact, us!

So, how do we avoid this little mind trick? For starters, we can take the time to envision our future self, take their advice, and apply it *in the present*. In the movie *Back to the Future Part II*, the character Biff travels 60 years back in time to give his younger self an almanac containing records of major sporting events for the past 50 or so years. He instructs his younger self to "use this so you can start winning."

While Biff's motives were dubious, we can use this knowledge to bet on our future self in positive ways. To do this, we need to forecast this future version of ourselves—their wants, desires, what they're up to—allowing that future self to dictate the way we feel and the actions we take in the here and now. Research shows that the more connected we are to our future self, the more likely we are to be motivated to take action today that will positively impact us down the road.

HOW TO DO IT

1. **Envision your future self.** Picture your future self in a beautiful, positive light. What do you look like? What sort of actions do you take? What does your future self believe in? What do you do in the face of a challenge? Who do you like being around? What inspires you? How do you stick to positive habits? What

have you accomplished? Use these writing prompts as examples or feel free to come up with your own. Journal all the thoughts that come up for you when you picture your future self.

2. **Familiarize yourself with your future you.** In order to move toward that ideal future self, keep your mind focused on that person. Read your journal entry in the morning and before you go to sleep at night. Add to it when you're feeling inspired. Familiarize yourself with this awesome individual *who just happens to be you*!

3. **Act "as if."** Now it's time to try your future self on for size. Take one or two actions that your future self might take. If those actions feel both exciting and slightly nerve-racking, you're right on track.

#3 Find Reprieve When You Breathe

WHY IT WORKS

You're going carb-free when your favorite lasagna makes an entrance out of the kitchen, inching closer *and closer* to you—the saucy enticer. Your heart skips a beat. A bead of sweat forms on your brow. Yet, instead of grabbing the serving pan and emptying it onto your plate, you wink at that sultry dish—and use your invisible secret willpower weapon instead: your breath!

And not just *any* breath: *diaphragmatic breathing*—a powerful type of deep breathing where your diaphragm contracts and your belly expands. It's a type of breathing that helps with emotional balance—i.e., enhancing your ability to *keep calm and carry on*— even when confronted by an Italian temptress or the like.

Health psychologist Kelly McGonigal advocates for this type of breathing, sharing in her book *The Willpower Instinct* that slowing your breathing down to "four to six breaths per minute" is one amazing way to "immediately boost willpower" and shift "the brain and body from a state of stress to self-control mode."

So! When you're feeling tempted or drained, remember that you may just be one deep breath away from regaining willpower.

HOW TO DO IT

Go low and think slow. When we're stressed, our breath becomes shallow, emanating from our chest. Instead, focus on breathing from the belly and slowing down your breath. You can start by simply having an awareness of how you're breathing: Place one hand on your chest and the other just above your navel, so you can feel your diaphragm—instead of your chest—moving with each breath. Inhale and exhale slowly and fully.

#4 Let Go of Ego

WHY IT WORKS

When we were just six, seven, or eight months old and first learning to crawl, we most likely didn't dart our eyes over at little Bobby—three weeks younger than us, yet somehow sliding across the floor like a pro—and think, behind faint, furrowed baby brows, "Better out-crawl this tiny tike today." Yet, in today's world of social media, followers, celebrations, announcements, cultural demands, professional demands, and likes, it can be tempting to feel like we always need to be winning, achieving, and doing—seamlessly and beautifully at that.

In her book *Mindset*, Carol Dweck describes a group of kids who were given difficult puzzles to solve. They weren't exactly solving them. Yet, despite their lack of progress, these children were still, surprisingly, excited and inspired. One 10-year-old boy smacked his lips while shouting, "I love a challenge!" Another proclaimed, "You know, I was *hoping* this would be informative!"

Dweck was positively puzzled, wondering *what was wrong with them*? "You coped with failure or you didn't cope with failure," she'd assumed. Then it hit her. When the kids landed on a problem they didn't understand, they didn't think they were failing. "They thought they were learning," she writes.

They say there's a lot we can learn from children. Imagine if, like these kids, we truly didn't *see* failing. Imagine if we saw problems as opportunities to become more informed. Resilient. Inspired. Opportunities to *love learning*.

When we prioritize our ego and operate from that *fixed mindset*, every chance we have to exert willpower becomes about succeeding or failing and what each outcome might say about our "specialness" or innate talent. On the other hand, when we lean into a *growth mindset*, progress becomes about enjoying and learning from the process. It becomes about strengthening our ability with each success and each failure, and seeing "failures" as learning experiences. It becomes about growing and course correcting along the way.

That said, taking inventory of what's working versus what's not, what's helping us skirt temptation or successfully complete that task, is important! But, equating our results with our ability—looking for them to prove or disprove something inherent about us—is a good way to get down, not leap, not crawl, not even inch forward toward what we want.

HOW TO DO IT

1. **Remember the growth versus fixed mindset.** If you find yourself erring on the side of "fixed mindset," simply notice it. Then think: What would a growth-mindset response to this temptation, setback, or challenge look like?

2. **Make it an experiment.** If you fall seven times, then decide to stay down, you'll never know whether you could've gotten up on that eighth try. Experiment with what might trip you up, then keep on rising.

3. **Don't get down, get curious.** Whether you succeed or succumb to temptation, ask yourself why. What led to "accomplishing" and what led to "giving in"?

#5 Curb Your Confirmation Bias

WHY IT WORKS

Let's say you're on this new healthy eating kick. It feels great. You're all "Dressing on the side, please!" when out to dinner and saying, "Let's halve the recipe!" in the kitchen. But you haven't told your husband, because you sense he'll doubt your ability to stick to it. When you finally tell him, he responds, "That's great! Let's see what happens."

"I knew it!" you think to yourself, assuming your husband is being sarcastic and undermining your resolve. But, perhaps your husband is actually looking forward to seeing you in better health. This is confirmation bias, where we cherry-pick information that supports our pre-existing beliefs or worldview. Perhaps your husband *was* enthused about your plan. Or, maybe he *did* actually question your ability. Regardless of the truth, if we aim to understand where we may be biased, we can gain a fresh perspective and open ourselves up to more positive possibilities.

HOW TO DO IT

1. **Take a step back.** Biases may feel hard to recognize because we're typically entrenched in them, so take a step back and look at yourself objectively. Even try using the illeism technique in strategy #20 on page 54. What biases might you have that confirm a viewpoint that won't help you progress? First dates are always bad? If there's a carb in the room, I'm going to eat it? Is this an absolute fact?

2. **Look from another angle.** Pause and ask yourself whether there's an alternative viewpoint available. What might a dating coach or dietitian say? Would they agree with you?

3. **Challenge yourself to new thinking.** We can always follow our confirmation bias and keep going the same way. Or we can challenge ourselves to believe something new and different. It might feel strange at first, but if it supports us in forward progress, it's worth trying.

Go for "Old"

Want to invest in your future? Start by investing in an age-progressed rendering of yourself! Not your typical investment advice, I know. Yet the reason we forgo our healthy eating plan or our New Year's resolutions may be because it's tough for us humans to relate to or empathize with our future self (see strategy #2 on page 25).

Researchers found one interesting solution. In several laboratory studies, participants' self-control regarding hypothetical savings decisions increased after seeing age-progressed renderings of themselves! After viewing their virtual future self, participants across the board held off on accepting monetary rewards in the present, saving them for the future instead. Cool, huh?

So, if you want to strengthen motivation around your long-term goals, check out an app like AgingBooth, FaceApp, or Oldify, and speed up your aging process (virtually) to make better choices now (in real life).

#6 Set Intentions

WHY IT WORKS

A client of mine—we'll call her Marla—valued going to the gym and spending time alone. When Marla had adequate "alone time" to read or reflect, she felt at ease. If she made it to the gym at least three times a week, she felt physically and mentally satiated.

However, Marla noticed she wasn't getting these needs met lately. Her family and friends would invite her out, or her boss would ask her to complete a last-minute task, and more often than not, she'd accept their request. This left her in a mental tug-of-war. On the one hand, Marla was happy to spend time with friends and feel valued by her boss, but on the other, she was frustrated not to be able to satisfy her own needs, too.

She initially believed that connecting with friends and exercising were equally important. But eventually, Marla realized if she didn't work out, she wouldn't enjoy that time with friends as much, particularly if she compromised her own needs for theirs.

To help Marla remedy this, we worked together to pinpoint what was *most important to her* and identify *which* circumstances were worth prioritizing, such as working out and spending time on her own. Next, we implemented if-then statements to make it easier for her to say no to plans or simply know how to best respond to different options. *If* (for instance) she had a good friend's birthday to celebrate, *then* she'd sacrifice her alone time, as she realized that celebrating a dear friend's birthday was something that was, in fact, more important to her than her other solo needs.

These seemingly simple if-then statements are furtively powerful this way, as they help you decide how you'll handle impulses, temptations, and conflicting needs ahead of time so you're not stuck decision-making on the spot. In fact, according to more than 200 studies, if-then statements help increase goal attainment and productivity by an average of 200 to 300 percent.

HOW TO DO IT

1. **Plan in advance.** Brainstorm potential deterrents or conflicts to successfully implementing your willpower habit strategies. Write down any typical distractions or impulses that might prevent you from progressing, such as being asked to brunch when you're supposed to be cleaning the kitchen or being offered an alcoholic beverage when you were planning not to drink.

2. **Implement if-then statements.** Think up potential if-then statements before going out or starting your week. For example: *If* I'm asked to attend brunch on Sunday, *then* I'll clean the kitchen before I go. *If* I'm offered a glass of wine, *then* I'll ask for a Diet Coke instead.

#7 Celebrate Negative Emotions

WHY IT WORKS

While striving toward your goal, do you ever encounter emotions you'd rather avoid—worry, doubt, anxiousness, discouragement? Naturally, when we're in the thick of these negative emotions, it's easy to make them mean something negative, such as "I'm just not capable." It's the positive emotions—excitement, optimism, confidence—that signify we're on track and cut out for the task at hand. Right?

Here's some good news for when you're not feeling so good. Experiencing negative emotions actually indicates that we're right where we should be. Think about it! The operative word in *trying something new* is *trying*. Striving, endeavoring, going for it. Instead of seeing the struggle as a sign that we're behind, or even incompetent, let it indicate what it really is: simply experiencing the feelings that come with doing something we're not yet used to. If you're feeling challenged, you're doing it right.

HOW TO DO IT

Define the true meaning. Try tuning into your emotions while endeavoring to reach your goal. If you feel worry or frustration, consider what you're making those feelings mean. Is it "Yay! This means I'm striving toward my goal!" or "Yikes! I should throw in the towel on my willpower habit"? If you're making them mean the latter, remind yourself of the purpose of these more challenging emotions. If you're experiencing them, you're right where you should be, so accept them as part of the mission. If you weren't trying, you wouldn't be feeling them.

#8 Prevent Procrastination

WHY IT WORKS

You drum your fingertips on your laptop, all set to write that report. But first you decide to quickly post that tweet, send that text, or do laundry while you're writing, too, and—uh oh! Out of detergent? One quick trip to the drugstore, then five hours later your Christmas shopping is done and it's July. *Anyone?*

Ah, procrastination: that beguiling friend who urges us to postpone those not-so-fun activities in lieu of what feels more exciting, or simply achievable in the moment.

And that's the thing. Procrastination may stem from simply not seeing a clear-cut path to successful implementation. If we're overwhelmed by multiple options or varying methods, if we don't know where to start or how to proceed, it's understandable that we'd want to direct our attention to something easier.

How can we finish the race if we don't know where the starting line is?

By creating, scheduling, and following a plan, though, we can reduce procrastination and support "the enactment of difficult actions," according to "Beyond Willpower: Strategies for Reducing Failures of Self-Control," a study by research psychologists from Harvard and the University of Pennsylvania. These things also help with forgetfulness, too.

Once you take action and follow the steps laid out for you, you finally create freedom from those back-and-forth thoughts: Can I really do this? Will I stick to it? Instead, you have an answer. A solid timeline. A direct path to your goal. Start with step one, and from there it's simply one foot in front of the other.

HOW TO DO IT

Use SMART goals (see page 18) to:

1. **Decide on an achievable goal.**

2. **Create daily and/or weekly "subgoals" along the way.**

3. **Calendar your plan and remember you can course correct as needed.**

4. **Celebrate progress and wins! Define what these things are for you.**

#9 Prioritize Action over Results

WHY IT WORKS

Many of the clients I work with operate under the belief that the harder they are on themselves, the more likely they are to succeed. This assumption is a relatively common one. However, the tendency to come from a "Do it, or else!" perspective often triggers more avoidance than action. Plus, besides just "doing it," they also *must* do it well. How's that for pressure? Perfectionism and procrastination tend to go hand in hand this way. Except that when dancing with this fun little duo, nothing ever really shakes out. Instead, perfectionist thinking leaves many in a cycle of avoidance, then last-minute addressing and stressing.

To get anywhere, we have to get going. So! Instead of prioritizing results (and perfect ones at that), make the goal to stay in motion by taking consistent, imperfect, action steps.

HOW TO DO IT

1. **Choose an action.** Decide what action would feel like a success to you. If you're applying to new jobs, successful actions might include first steps like researching companies, working on your résumé, and networking, as opposed to actually landing the job. Of course, a result like getting hired would be fantastic!

2. **Act on it!** By making success mean *action* over *avoidance* and *progress* over *perfection*, we open ourselves up to possibility and opportunity. This, ultimately, can strengthen our willpower muscle much more than equating winning with receiving an offer letter—and, with enough practice developing our skills and resilience, that offer letter may be more likely to land in our inbox.

#10 Expect Great Things

WHY IT WORKS

If we want to walk but expect to crawl, will we walk? If we want to earn but expect not to, will we make money?

Dr. Jennice Vilhauer shares something rather remarkable about us humans in an article in *Psychology Today*. We tend to "act on what we expect, not what we want." So, if we ever really wanted to succeed or wanted to quit a habit but—deep down—didn't expect to, we might have ended up unsuccessful. If that was the case, it's not because we didn't really want the change. It's because our actions reflected our negative expectations as opposed to our real desires. Fascinating, right?

Our expectations are often informed by past experiences—what we know to be true about us, our ability, other people, and life in general—*up until this point*. But we cannot know what hasn't yet occurred. So, if we're trying to base more positive future expectations on more negative past experiences, we're going to remain stagnant.

How do we achieve what we want if we don't expect our wants to materialize?

The answer: Changing our expectations. Letting our future "ideal self" dictate our current standards. Letting our past expectations remain in the past. Deciding—in the present—that we're going to expect a new, different, positive, bountiful, exciting, even surreal next few days, months, and decades to come.

Let's decide to expect what we want and want what we expect.

HOW TO DO IT

1. **Notice your current expectations for yourself and others and question how your past experiences may have informed those ideas.** If you don't expect yourself to ace an exam, for example, how have past circumstances encouraged that prediction?

2. **Build new expectations from your future self (see strategy #2 on page 25).** If your "ideal" future self were to get what they wanted, what sort of expectations would they have set for themselves? In what way would they treat themselves or others? What experiences would they say yes or no to? Begin living into those future expectations and getting what you want in the here and now.

Take It from MJ

Earlier, I mentioned Michael Jordan and the fact that he always seemed to just *do*. Just succeed. Just dunk. Just magically outplay the opposing team.

Had I been more of a basketball fan, I might have known this wasn't exactly true.

"I've missed more than 9,000 shots in my career," begins his now famous quote, originally recorded in a 1990s Nike advertisement. "I've lost almost 300 games. Twenty-six times I've been trusted to take the game-winning shot and missed. I've failed over and over and over again in my life. And that is why I succeed."

What can MJ and his view on success teach us? Well, for starters, it's *not* all graceful wins and championship trophies. It's not back-to-back slam dunks each quarter. It's valiant efforts among failed attempts. It's getting back in the game after being sidelined. It's, as MJ says, "when you expect great things of yourself before you can do them."

#11 Let In the Light

WHY IT WORKS

Lemonade stands, inner tubes, increased willpower, SPF—*skrrt!* One of these does not look like the others (and it's not the sunblock). Believe it or not, the sun can get you tan (and focused!), so if you're lazin' by the pool, you might want to bring your beach towel *and* write your memoir.

When we're exposed to the sun, our levels of serotonin increase, which leads to a better mood. Yay! If we read strategy #55 (see page 117), we know that a shift in our mood toward optimism and excitement can lead to a shift in willpower toward increased attention. A recent study in *Environmental Health* showed that besides being a natural "mood enhancer," bright lights that mimicked the sun had an impact on people's attention.

In addition to increased attention, light enhances both alertness and performance during nighttime and daytime, and it also influences regional brain function.

Meaning that if you find yourself at the beach, pool, or simply sitting outdoors, you may have more than one reason to let the sunshine, *the sunnnnnshine in!*

HOW TO DO IT

1. **If you don't live in a location where there's sun all year round, invest in a light-therapy lamp.** This type of bright light mimics the sun, and you can use it at home or bring it to the office for an extra dose of sunshine.

2. **Find ways to make your home or office sunny.** Open the window shades when possible and invest in an antiglare screen protector for your computer.

#12 Feel the "Feels" Ahead of Time

WHY IT WORKS

When it comes to our goals, it's not actually the *result* we want most—it's the *feeling* we assume attaining the result will give us. So, if we want to be healthier, financially fit, or involved in an intimate relationship, what we *really* desire is a specific *feeling*, such as "energized," "competent," or "connected."

Many of us believe we need to achieve our goal to experience those feelings. The truth? Feeling those feelings first—and actively choosing to feel them often and regardless of our circumstances—positions us to reach our goals faster.

HOW TO DO IT

1. **Envision yourself achieving.** Decide the result you most desire and write it down. Now picture yourself attaining it. Take five to 10 minutes, close your eyes, and imagine yourself accomplishing your goal.

2. **Identify and describe your feelings.** When you picture yourself achieving your goal, how do you feel? Excited? Accomplished? Relieved? Journal the feelings you believe you'll have once you reach your objective.

3. **Experience your desired feelings now.** You don't have to wait until you achieve your goal to experience those feelings. Take the feeling of pleasure, for instance. Wrap yourself in a warm blanket, watch a baby laughing on YouTube—notice how pleasure is immediately at hand. Choose to feel pleasure in connection with various parts of your life, including reaching your goal. Viewing your goal in that positive light and taking positive action toward your goal will likely result in experiencing the process as pleasurable—and help you achieve your goal faster.

#13 Embrace an Attitude of Gratitude

WHY IT WORKS

When you think *gratitude*, do you picture someone who finds appreciation in the tiniest of things? For whom canceled flights and thunderstorms are somehow blessings in disguise? For whom joy is just as easily found in an Excel spreadsheet as in a Sunday brunch?

Are people who practice gratitude living in an alternate reality? Or are they *onto* something? As it turns out, gratitude isn't some "soft" practice for the faint of heart. To actively and consistently appreciate the good (*and* the bad *and* the ugly) takes work!

Our brain is wired to focus on the negative. Back in the day, when the physical environment posed many dangers, our negative focus made sense. Admiring a butterfly when a lion was pursuing us meant we'd, literally, be dead meat.

In today's world, our mind says, "Look out!" when we don't get enough social media likes. *Dear brain, reminder! It's the 21st century. My computer doesn't bite.*

How do we teach our brain the difference between a computer screen (a nonthreat) and a tiger (a real threat) so we don't fight or flight and dip into a negative focus so often?

The answer? Adopting an attitude of gratitude, which according to a 2016 study in the journal *Emotion*, "has recently been identified as a candidate emotion that supports self-control."

HOW TO DO IT

1. **Create prompts for moments of gratitude.** These might be questions like "What am I excited about today?" and "What do I love about my best friend?"

2. **Create a gratitude schedule.** Decide when you will answer your gratitude questions!

#14 Ask the Right Q's

WHY IT WORKS

If you wear a tube top and short shorts on a snowy day, there is a strong likelihood that you'll be cold. If you wait until Monday morning to fill your SUV with gas, there is a strong likelihood that you'll be late to your early-morning meeting! If we ask ourselves disempowering, uninspired questions, there is a strong likelihood that we'll be unmotivated and answerless. Pretty self-explanatory, right?

Yet, it's easy to have thoughts like "Will I cheat on my diet today?" or "Will I ever actually quit smoking?" And my personal favorite: "Do I suck?"

These are all dead-end questions that lead to dead-end answers. Yet, we try to answer them because they're the easiest to ask and the easiest to give a knee-jerk negative answer to: Of course you'll cheat. Nope, you'll never quit. Yes, you do totally suck.

So not cool, brain!

Particularly when we're feeling discouraged, this tricky little mind of ours may generate questions that keep us down. So, how are we supposed to come up with positive answers? Great question! And not to answer a question with a question, but what if there was a different way? A way to formulate empowering, motivational, thought-provoking questions that uplift us? Inspire us? Actually help us find real solutions?

The power lies in the open-ended question.

Question: How do open-ended questions help us?
Answer: They prompt our brain to think of possibility—to come up with solutions, workarounds, and new ideas.
Question: Are closed-ended questions bad?
Answer: Yes.

See that? The closed-ended Q didn't even get a chance to state its case! Let's try that again.

Question: How do closed-ended questions differ from open-ended ones?

Answer: Closed-ended questions lead to closed-ended answers: yes or no. Right or wrong. Good or bad. Meaning limited options and less possibility. Instead, what might it be like to try asking more open-ended questions?

HOW TO DO IT

1. **Reframe your questions.** If you notice yourself asking closed-ended questions—like "Will I get it done?" or "Will I make them mad?"—decide how you can reframe those Q's to something that doesn't yield a simple yes or no answer. Some examples are "What can I do to get excited about today?" and "How can I put myself in their shoes?" and "If I knew I would feel good and be successful, how would that change the process for me?"

2. **Work on noticing when you're asking yourself questions that keep you stuck.** We might default to something like "Why am I asking myself these negative questions?" Instead, try "How can I start trying this open-ended question thing?"

3. **Get to answering them!** You can journal or even just say the answer aloud to yourself. Or get a coach! Coaches are trained to ask empowering questions and determine what's keeping you stuck (see the sidebar "Hire a Coach," page 109).

#15 *Immerse Yourself in Nature*

WHY IT WORKS

Before diving into this strategy, earmark this page and go pop a squat next to a peace lily (or the nearest greenery). According to attention restoration theory, or ART, being in nature—the trees, the ocean, the sand—or even sitting next to a potted plant can help us focus better.

In a 2015 study based on ART, 150 students looked out the window at either a flowering-meadow green roof or a bare concrete roof for 40 seconds straight. Participants who stopped to view the flowers demonstrated an increased ability to concentrate on a subsequent task. They made fewer errors on that task than their "bare roof beholder" cohorts.

So, how does *that* work? As it turns out, viewing nature—grass, mountains, shrubbery—even for a short period of time increases parasympathetic activity, leading to decreased anxiety, increased relaxation, and positive emotional states. And as shown by this roof study, taking a microbreak to view nature can be restorative and an attention booster. "This study showed us that looking at an image of nature for less than a minute was all it took to help people perform better on our task," shares University of Melbourne research fellow Kate Lee.

That's right—a mere image of nature will do the trick. So, if your office is devoid of greenery, just flip through March to July of your coworker's flora and fauna calendar. Or grab your paintbrushes and cue up Bob Ross on YouTube.

HOW TO DO IT

1. **Carve out time in nature.** You don't have to build a greenhouse or even invest in a plant. Simply find times during the day when you can go for a walk outside or look at something that isn't

artificial. In other words, something that came straight from Mother Nature—a plant, a flower, a stream. Even touching sand can help you increase your attention.

2. **Seek imagery.** Can't find anything nature-made to focus on? Check out that photo of a tree you captured on your phone, or make your desktop screensaver a mountain or stream. Listen to soundscapes featuring a babbling brook or birds in the rain forest. Plant that seed for increasing your focus.

Believe Your Willpower Is Limitless

Imagine you've put in a really demanding day of work. The next morning, how do you feel?

___ Drained, my willpower is depleted.
___ Perfectly fine, I'm ready to dive into work again.

How you answered this question may depend on your current view of willpower. Research by Swiss psychologists Katharina Bernecker and Veronika Job suggests that, particularly after a demanding day, people's beliefs about willpower predict their ability to perform and their actual performance.

Based on a study of 157 university students, the researchers concluded that people who believe that their willpower is limited:

1. Expect to make less progress in unpleasant tasks,
2. Expect to be more exhausted from unpleasant tasks,
3. And are less effective in striving toward goals . . .

. . . than people who believe that their willpower is not limited. In fact, people with a nonlimited belief actually felt a positive effect from demands on their self-control, which further energized their willpower.

#16 Reimagine Temptations

WHY IT WORKS

Let's talk temptation! The feeling of relief when inhaling that cigarette. The ooey-gooey first bite into a warm homemade cookie. When we paint these things that way, they become it. But when we attribute new connotations to the things that trigger us, although the actual object doesn't change, our ideas about them do.

Remember the marshmallow experiment back in chapter 1? According to psychologist Walter Mischel, when children were encouraged to think of the marshmallows as "fluffy white clouds" they were able to wait more than twice as long to eat them—as opposed to the children imagining the "sticky and sweet" taste of those same treats, who, not surprisingly, indulged quicker.

If the labels we ascribe to things tend to shape the way we view them, why not just label indulgences in a way that minimizes their temptation?

Picture a cigarette as a "teeth-decaying stick" that "gives our mouths wrinkles." Anything that shines a negative light on the experience. Anything that *repels* instead of *compels* you.

HOW TO DO IT

Reimagine the habits you begrudgingly enjoy. If you bite your nails consistently, check out an unpleasant video of other nail biters. Each time you're tempted to bite your nails, play it. In doing so, you're giving your mind an alternate way to view that same activity you once labeled "enticing." The more you can associate the neutral or negative new thought with that habit, the less desirable that habit will become over time.

#17 Make It Mean Something

WHY IT WORKS

Many of the clients and colleagues I work with are striving toward something. Creating more impact in others' lives. Getting that promotion. Arguing less with their wife. Quitting social media. All of these goals require them to do things a little differently—think differently, problem-solve differently, react differently—to get different results. Now, many of us hear *different* and assume it means *difficult*. But what if instead of being difficult, it was refreshing, stimulating, thought provoking?

What if *different* was an opportunity to learn, grow, become more of the person we truly are? Who we're truly meant to be? Instead of viewing the process of change as one we *have* to do, by finding ways of *wanting* to do it, we can make it way more, well, doable.

How? By making it *mean something.*

One of my clients trained five days a week for months for a marathon she didn't qualify for. This could have really upset her. She had put in so much effort. She had worked *so* hard. But she wasn't upset. She chose to see the denial as evidence that she'd stepped outside her comfort zone. She saw it as an opportunity to bounce back after "failure."

She didn't see *rejection*. She saw *redirection*. Later that year, she trained for another marathon in Japan. And she qualified.

Imagine that perhaps unforeseen challenges aren't ill-timed obstacles you now have to overcome, but perfectly placed opportunities you get to grow from. What if they weren't happening to you, but for you? It might be challenging to consider that what we label as "bad" might potentially be helping us. But why not try? If it works, there'll be fewer "bad" things and more things! Some, perhaps, good!

HOW TO DO IT

1. **Ask yourself two questions.** If this experience is somehow helping you, in what way is that? If you were always meant to face this obstacle, why might that be? You may come up with "Nada, there's no reason," "This sucks," or "Is Aliya kidding me with this?" I'm not kidding, but I get your reaction. This is new and different!

2. **Answer the questions.** Consider this a challenge in creativity—you're ascribing different meaning to the way you view that obstacle. Journal your answers to get the wheels turning. Instead of saying, "I don't know," ask yourself what you'd answer if you did know. My hunch is that, deep down, you do. And that might just put it all into perspective.

#18 Forgo Decision Fatigue

WHY IT WORKS

You know all those tiny, relatively mindless choices we make every day? The blue button-down or the flannel? Take the kids to daycare, then get coffee, or vice versa? Three Splendas or two? Now or later? Yes or no? When we add up the time we spend deciding—pro and con listing, weighing the options—all those seemingly insignificant deliberations can, in fact, wear us down.

There's actually a scientific term for this, aptly named *decision fatigue.* It might be the reason you give in and just say "yes, okay" to buying your toddler the toy, or why that wisecrack about your daughter-in-law's cooking slipped out when you'd been trying to be better at restraint. *It's the fatigue, I swear!*

Decision fatigue happens when you've spent a lot of time making choices, so at the end of the day the quality of your decisions is negatively impacted. Well, it doesn't literally always occur at the end of the day, just at the tail end of a long decision-making session.

But instead of haphazardly handling the unexpected, expect to have decisions handled—ahead of time.

HOW TO DO IT

1. **Decide ahead of time.** In a *New York Times* article, American journalist John Tierney writes, "People with the best self-control are the ones who structure their lives so as to conserve willpower." So! The good news is that in order to be awesome at self-control, it's less "have willpower" and more "have a calendar"—and don't forget to use it. How cool is that? It means if we focus on structuring our days for success and sticking to our scheduled plans, we no longer need to look to some inner willpower reserve for help. We can simply look to our calendar

instead. Fill your calendar and make decisions ahead of time, including decisions on the things you can't always plan for. Use the if-then statements you learned in strategy #6 (see page 32).

2. **Take a break.** Take planned breaks, or if you need to take an unplanned one, plan where you'll go. Will you take a walk? Meditate? Make a break part of your routine to reclaim willpower.

#19 Work Out for Willpower

WHY IT WORKS

Not turning into a couch potato is important. The remedy? Exercise, healthy eating, maintaining good habits—you know, the usual suspects. But if you're looking to achieve more than just "not becoming one with the couch," there's good reason to consider exercise—especially if you'd also like to procrastinate less, feel more motivated, and even save more and spend less. It's true! Working out can help with all those things, including making your bank account happy.

In a four-month study, a group of nonexercisers found themselves at the gym. The participants were assessed at monthly intervals. After engaging in a program of regular exercise, participants experienced positive regulatory behaviors such as better study habits and monitoring of spending, and a decrease in perceived stress and less alcohol and caffeine consumption were reported.

Another two-part experiment looked at the effects of exercise on those who were overweight or sedentary, specifically measuring their ability to delay gratification. Even an entire month after their training had ended, even after they had stopped going to the gym, participants reported experiencing an increase in self-control.

So, if you find yourself bench-pressing or bar-belling, you are simultaneously strengthening more than just your muscles!

HOW TO DO IT

1. **Break free from unhelpful thoughts.** I've worked with many clients who've felt they were simply "perpetually unmotivated." It's time to eradicate that false belief right here, right now. There's nothing that differentiates you from an avid gym goer other than that they've simply *been in the habit* of working out.

If you haven't exercised recently, you merely *haven't built a habit of it* yet. When you start *building*, you'll start *becoming*! That goes for any positive habit you might want to form.

2. **Shift your mentality.** Replace thoughts such as "I don't *have* enough energy to workout" with "I'm going to *gain* the energy I need *by working out*." It's like driving. You can't go until you press on the gas.

3. **Start small.** You don't have to sign up for a marathon or even exercise for 30 minutes a day. If you haven't worked out in a while, simply taking a walk is a perfect place to begin. Start small and take it one step at a time.

#20 *Step Out of Your Story*

WHY IT WORKS

When you're stuck between two choices—go to yoga or sleep in, splurge on the sweater or appreciate it through the window—try using illeism, the act of speaking about your experience in the third person.

For example, "Aliya hesitates to share this strategy because she wonders whether readers will find it silly."

See that—better already! Seriously though, ruminating over a choice, particularly when under pressure, can lead to impaired judgment. Instead, creating a small amount of space between you and the story of what you're experiencing—simply by speaking about it in the third person—can help you view it without biases. It may even help you exert self-control when faced with tempting options in the short term.

HOW TO DO IT

1. **Recognize the rumination.** When you find yourself in a pickle—contemplating whether you'll follow or deviate from your willpower plan—avoid the rumination trap of "should I or shouldn't I" eat the brownie or not, or take time off work or not. When you can make a good case for multiple options, it's easy and tempting to seesaw back and forth.

2. **Use illeism for an instant new perspective on the story.** For example: "Amy is worried her boss won't value her if she takes time off." By self-distancing this way, we create room to observe and accept our feelings, which is one of the first steps to successfully enacting change.

Self-Distancing for Self-Regulation

When deciding whether to sign with the Cleveland Cavaliers or Miami Heat, basketball star LeBron James said, "One thing I didn't want to do was make an emotional decision. I wanted to do what's best for LeBron James and to do what makes LeBron James happy." In "Self-Talk as a Regulatory Mechanism: How You Do It Matters," researchers ponder whether James's "shift in tense" was simply a quirk of speech or James enacting illeism, purposefully speaking about oneself in the third person (see strategy #20, page 54).

When James referred to "LeBron James" that way, was it because he was just as impressed with himself as his fans? Or did he, in fact, use self-distancing for his own emotional benefit? Mystery aside, the fact remains that practicing illeism can actually improve decision-making in the moment, helping us regulate thoughts, feelings, and behaviors under stress by figuratively stepping outside of ourselves.

#21 Put New Habits on Autopilot

WHY IT WORKS

When behaviors become habits, we no longer have to ruminate over how to execute them. Think about it. After 40 years of driving, we don't hesitate while opening the car door, wipe sweat from our brow as we get behind the wheel, or reiterate to ourselves, "First, put the key in the ignition. Wait until you hear the engine. Now, foot on the left pedal, hand on the shift, check the rearview mirror . . ." We just drive!

Imagine "just driving" with all of our desired habits. Not contemplating going to the gym—just going. Not debating whether to indulge in the office donuts—just not eating them. Simply pumping the brakes on what we don't want and shifting what we do want into autopilot.

The secret to this gift is giving yourself what's called "activation energy," which according to author, speaker, and positive psychology advocate Shawn Achor, is that "initial spark needed to catalyze a reaction." In this case, it's the spark that jump-starts a positive habit and moves us past our inertia.

"If you can make a habit 20 seconds easier to start, the likelihood of doing it rises dramatically," Achor says, aptly calling this the "20-second rule."

Want to exercise in the morning? Put your sneakers and socks beside your bed, so in the a.m. all you have to do is slip them on—or sleep in your gym clothes like Achor! He actually uses all these tips, which he says makes him likelier to do those early-morning workouts.

Now, for you, it may look less like "sleep in my sports bra" and more like "leave the French fluency book on the living room table and hide the Xbox controller." On the flip side, creating a 20-second delay on certain activities, such as taking the batteries out of the remote (meaning you'd have to find them and put them back in), has been proven to dramatically decrease TV watching.

HOW TO DO IT

Set yourself up. Brainstorm simple ways of making it easier to engage in what you want and walk away from what you don't. Falling asleep without washing your face at night? #NoJudgment! Leave the face wash in your bathroom sink in the morning so at night it's there, waiting for you. Consider it a mini intervention. From yourself, for yourself!

#22 Befriend Your Inner Critic

WHY IT WORKS

Let's talk about our inner critic: that overly critical, demanding, even demeaning voice in our head that tells us things like "You're too old for this, you should have started eating healthy decades ago!" or "These strategies won't work for you, you'll never stick to them!" The inner critic has a strong mission: put us in self-doubt and make us feel guilty, incompetent, or even ashamed. And it doesn't act alone. It sometimes brings its cousin, "compare and despair," who'll have us comparing ourselves to others, then despairing over our supposed inadequacy. Or it'll invite old "imposter syndrome," the resident intimidator who'll make us feel inadequate despite success. Quite the stand-up family!

Now, the tricky thing about the inner critic is its characterizations often *feel* true. One of my client's inner critics would tell her, "You never get your work done on time!" and "You're a procrastinator—that won't change!" She could very easily have believed her inner critic, because its taunts always seemed rather spot-on. She could easily have found evidence for why her inner critic was right about her. She didn't always keep an ideal pace when it came to her work. She wasn't always satisfied with her efforts. If she chose to agree with her critic's depictions of her, she'd likely feel defeated and want to throw in the towel.

So, how do we stop this little rascal? Observing it is a great place to start. Picture a spotlight shining onto a stage and suddenly veering left, directly onto an actor in the wings. This actor didn't want to be seen, as he was taunting other actors on stage and they didn't know where the noise was coming from. Once the actor has been revealed, imagine him strutting out onto the stage and proclaiming, "You found me! Joke's over!"

Picture our inner critic *the same way*. By shining a light on it, by just noticing it, we can diminish its intensity, even act in spite of it. We can hear its seemingly logical pleas to stop us from progressing and quit taking action and go hide under the covers instead. Or we can interpret it as a kind of white noise or fly we can simply shoo away. We can move forward regardless of what it preaches, or even do something daring, like trying to understand its intentions.

Because the inner critic *is*, in fact, well intentioned. Particularly when you're engaged in something where there's a potential risk of "failure," the inner critic is going to say things to hold you back and keep you "in the cave."

Knowing this can help us relax or even soften our judgment of the inner critic. The inner critic is merely a misguided helper who actually wants to keep us safe and out of harm's way. But in doing so, it's unknowingly inflicting more harm than creating good. The inner critic is a concept used in psychotherapy to describe that critical inner voice that badgers people. By experimenting with the following action steps, we can curb even our inner critic's best efforts.

HOW TO DO IT

1. **Recognize it.** How do we rid ourselves of this misguided helper? This inner judge? We don't. But by recognizing it's there, we can progress, succeed, and accomplish despite it.

2. **Personify it.** Picture your inner critic. Is it big, little, green, purple? Does it look like a little monster or alien? By personifying our inner critic, we can more easily visualize it, enabling us to observe and gain distance from it instead of buying into its jeers.

3. **Befriend it.** When my inner critic starts up, I try telling it, "Thanks for trying to protect me, but I don't need you right now."

#23 Rise and Shine!

WHY IT WORKS

Picture this. It's Monday morning. You arrive at your office, sit at your desk, and dive headfirst into tackling those expense reports and preparing overdue proposals. You schedule your workload for the next six months all before your morning coffee. Typical workday? Or an episode of *The Twilight Zone*?

For a majority of us, 8:00 a.m. looks more like responding to e-mails, skimming the news, scrolling through Instagram, and *then* starting our more challenging to-dos. Post coffee.

Here's a helpful hint. Our mental energy, or "brain power," is at its peak during the first two to four hours after we wake up, according to Duke University psychologist Dan Ariely. Experts like Roy Baumeister similarly affirm self-control is strongest in the morning.

Meaning if you've been feeling lethargic or lack the drive to complete a task, it very well may have more to do with timing than anything else. #WhenIt'sTheClockNotYou!

HOW TO DO IT

1. **Think about your schedule the night before.** Pick one or two tasks that require the most mental energy or creativity. Then determine the time it will take to complete each task. Block out time in the morning for each one (see strategy #29, page 70).

2. **Before settling into work, prep your environment.** For example, alert potential distractors you'll be unavailable from 8:00 to 11:00 a.m. Turn your phone on silent, and plan to check e-mails later in the morning (see strategy #37, page 86).

3. **Find ways to minimize distractions and expand your opportunity to stay on task and remain productive.** We have more control over our environment than we may think, so let's get creative!

#24 *Create Calm*

WHY IT WORKS

I once had a client, let's call her Jane, who found it difficult to have productive conversations with her mother. What made the conversations tedious for Jane was that she'd go into them assuming her mother would disagree with her on most every topic—from work to relationships. Her goal was to forge connection with her mother, but she'd become nervous, angry, or anxious—ultimately finding herself unable to endure the conversation. Through our work together, Jane realized that to get anywhere she had to start by prioritizing her own emotional well-being, before addressing her self-identified inability to remain calm during these discussions.

What does this tell us about willpower? Well, many of our most important decisions are made under stress, and acute stress—like what Jane experienced—may impair our ability to self-regulate or control our emotions.

So, how did Jane combat this? By *creating calm*.

By helping my client find ways to "come to calm" both before and during her conversations with her mother, we were able to change the way she showed up for these encounters. Jane became ready to do her part to attempt to achieve a different outcome, or at least experience the conversations from a place of clarity, as opposed to confusion and upset.

HOW TO DO IT

1. **Practice diaphragmatic breathing.** Practice this technique from strategy #3 (see page 27) both before and during the conversation or the triggering circumstance.

2. **Decide how you want to show up ahead of time.** A mentor of mine once described how she loves people who are consistent. If they constantly do something like "get angry" or "become

critical," at least they do that consistently—so you know exactly what to expect from them! Although she may not be able to change her mother's response, Jane could plan for how she would act and what she would say in the face of heightened emotion. She could come from her "highest self."

#25 *Lower Other Life Stressors*

WHY IT WORKS

The way this book is written might have us feeling like we're playing defense, under the assumption that the *big bad temptation monster* is strong and oh-so-powerful. If—and only if—we wield our willpower *just right*, we might have a chance of thwarting it.

Instead of defending the castle, raising the drawbridge, and predicting we'll go to mental battle each time cookies are served or drinks are passed, let's switch to offense.

Let's get smart about the manner in which we specifically operate. At what time of day and under what circumstances are we most likely to be tempted? Beyond the willpower we're learning to cultivate, what else do we need in our lives to feel good? Content? Whole?

When our needs are met and our stress is down, sticking to our willpower habit can become relatively automatic. Instead of spending our time on guard, waiting to slay the temptation monster, we can form a relationship with it that works.

HOW TO DO IT

1. **Identify the needs most important to you.** Maslow's hierarchy of needs identifies basic, psychological, and self-fulfillment needs, ranging from health to intimacy to financial security and pursuing goals. What are your top needs? Adequate sleep? Playing music? Time with friends? Take some time to pinpoint what truly matters (see strategy #43, page 96).

2. **Carve out and schedule time each week to get those needs met.** If you identified sleep as a priority, set an alarm that tells you when to go to bed and when to wake up. If you are working

on a balance between alone time and socializing, set plans for the month in advance.

Find Your Peak for Productivity

If you believe you can fly but don't always reach your potential, you may want to reconsider the *time of day* you tackle projects. If you act like an owl, staying up working late into the night, but find it draining, it might be because you're actually a lark—that is, a morning person. These bird names—lark, owl, and "third bird"—are "chronotypes," and according to author Daniel Pink, they each represent different types of body clocks.

Per Pink's theory, larks (super early risers) and third birds (those who naturally wake between 8:00 and 10:00 a.m.) experience their daily energy levels as peak, trough, and rebound. Their peak ability to focus occurs around two hours after waking—their optimal time for productive work. For our owl friends, it's the reverse—they peak after dark.

If you've been expending energy without seeing results, don't wing it. Determine your type, soar toward success, and go ruffle some feathers.

#26 Get Comfortable with the Uncomfortable

WHY IT WORKS

As a child or even a teenager, if something didn't go our way and we got upset, even to the point of tears, we may have been told, "Buck up" or "Put on a happy face!" Perhaps we were offered a tissue to wipe away any sign of distress. Our parents or caretakers were likely well intentioned, seeking to spare us from those tough feelings and/or help us become "tough enough" to handle what life threw our way. This may have unintentionally taught us to avoid uncomfortable feelings, perhaps even at all costs. And ironically enough, sidestepping uncomfortable feelings actually *does* cost us—especially in the long run.

Now, does anyone *really* think to themselves, "Yay! My eyes are tearing up! Bring on the sadness!" or "Here comes the anger, woo-hoo!"? Not so much. Yet, if we were a tad friendlier to these not-so-fun emotional visitors, we'd lessen their impact and even strengthen our own willpower.

Think of it like this. Let's say we have two options: Eat the cookie and satisfy that craving, or resist instant gratification and satisfy our long-term healthy eating goal instead. If we want to resist eating the enticing cookie, we'll likely have to embrace the emotion of frustration or crankiness that comes with choosing resistance.

How's that for a mouthful? It comes down to this: Decidedly feeling those not-so-fun feelings is a tiny trick you can keep up your sleeve. Saying "Come on in!" when these emotional visitors show up—instead of slamming the door in their faces—actually works to your advantage.

It's like a piggy bank. Every time you feel uncomfortable yet still take the positive action, you're depositing a coin into your long-term goal account. The more coins you accrue, the stronger your willpower becomes, the more competence you gain, and the easier it becomes to save and demonstrate to yourself that you (yes, you!) are someone who *can*.

HOW TO DO IT

1. **Become aware.** What typically triggers you?

2. **Embrace the feeling of discomfort.** Identify it: "This is frustration" or "This is worry." Let yourself feel it.

3. **Act in the opposite direction.** Let the clammy palms, your mind urging you to eat the cookie, or the impulse to smoke actually remind you to run in the opposite direction. Consider this: When you feel tempted to eat the cookie, how will you remember to choose the salad instead?

#27 Forgo Fortune-Telling

WHY IT WORKS

Before beginning a new project, do you metaphorically consult your magic crystal ball to predict exactly how it will turn out? If you find yourself placing mental bets on outcomes, you might be engaging in fortune-telling, a cognitive distortion in which we negatively predict a future outcome without fact-checking its validity (see strategies #51 through #53, pages 110 to 115).

Our brain engages in this funny little thinking pattern because it thinks it's protecting us—determining every possible result so we'll never feel let down or caught off guard. Yet, in doing so, it causes unwanted stress in the here and now that can inhibit our willpower habit.

If you relate to this strategy, you're hardly alone. Let's find ways to alleviate fortune-telling and live in the moment so we don't have to spend our time trying to control the uncontrollable.

HOW TO DO IT

1. **Understand the payoff of worrying.** Even though by worrying we're mentally engaged in something "negative," there's always some positive payoff for why we're thinking or acting the way we are (see strategy #28, page 68). In this case, perhaps we're attempting to minimize expectations of success to prevent disappointment.

2. **Consider the impact.** Now, consider the ways fortune-telling is *negatively* impacting us. Perhaps by assuming we won't "get there," we're creating a sort of self-fulfilling prophecy.

3. **Shift your thinking.** What's a more pressure-free supportive thought you could embrace that doesn't *force* you to achieve your goal but still encourages action? For example, you might think, "Even though I'm not sure how this will turn out, I'm willing to try and stumble along the way." Practice and repeat that encouraging new thought.

#28 To Get Going, Find the Payoff of Staying Put

WHY IT WORKS

Want to curb your social media usage? Cut out overspending? Never bite your nails again? Maybe you've successfully paused these habits before, yet haven't completely committed to quitting. If that's you, you're hardly alone. So many of us keep the habits we say we're eager to get rid of and wind up stuck. But why might we do this, retain something we want to throw away? It turns out that in some way, shape, or form, holding on actually feels better than letting go. In other words, there's a payoff to staying put.

Now, you might be asking yourself, "How can I possibly be benefiting from sticking with a bad habit?" Yet when you think about it, if you haven't quit that habit yet, it's because that habit is, in some way, feeding you. When we identify and get curious about that reason or payoff—about the deeper ways that habit is benefiting you—we can finally embrace better habits and stop paying the piper! Although this payoff comes in different forms for different people, there are two that many identify with: fear of the unknown and fear of failure.

HOW TO DO IT

1. **Identify any resistance to the unknown.** By sticking with the cigarette-smoking, the overspending, and the nail-biting, we get to stay comfortable in the place we're familiar with. Even if we might not *love* it, at least we *know* it. Because for us humans, facing the unknown is downright difficult. Even if we understand that the alternative is healthier, it often feels better to simply continue that unideal habit. Let's embrace some honesty. What

fear-based thoughts do you have when you picture yourself succeeding at your new habit? For example: "I won't be able to stay consistent" or "What if my friends don't like the new me?" Jot these down.

2. **Practice mindfulness.** Next, recognize any feelings of resistance to change. Instead of running from them, embrace them. Where in your body do those feelings reside? Your chest? Your stomach? A feeling is merely a physical sensation. By making room for the feeling instead of pushing it away or denying it, we can move toward the new action we want to take with presence as opposed to resistance (see strategy #26, page 65).

3. **Identify any fear of failure.** What would you do if you knew you couldn't fail? Skydive? Run for president? Or maybe you'd set out to achieve the exact goal you're hoping this book will help with. Yet, if there was zero possibility of failure, how might you be doing things differently with regard to developing your willpower? Fear of failure robs us of the opportunity to try, let alone succeed. And if we never try, we'll never have to potentially face failure. We'll never have to be disappointed or face self-judgment. The payoff? Sparing yourself from those negative feelings.

4. **Redefine failure.** Give not trying the same connotation you might give failure. By applying more positive connotations with failure—a willingness to try, bravery, strength, courage, discipline—you'll help make the concept of failure more like a potential result of determination and positive effort expended. Instead of failure being a decree about your ability, it can be an example of your courage.

#29 Implement Time Blocking

WHY IT WORKS

When we have a million things on our plate, we can easily tackle a little of each at a time. The problem is this typically adds up to a whole lot of unfished tasks. Instead, by implementing time blocking, we alleviate the pressure of not knowing when we'll start or finish, or simply make progress on a project.

When you time-block, you set aside dedicated chunks of time to work exclusively on a specific task, creating uninterrupted space to complete that task fully. For example, from 12:00 to 1:00 p.m., I write. From 1:00 to 2:00 p.m., I eat. From 2:00 to 2:15 p.m., I meditate. The more specific you are with what you'll complete during the allotted time, the better. You might ask yourself, "How much will I write from 12:00 p.m. to 1:00 p.m.?" and "Will I cook or order takeout?" Initially, this tactic may sound restrictive. Yet, implementing time blocking helps us create freedom from the overwhelming indecision and uncertainty that comes with simply working on tasks at will or haphazardly. Not to mention, time blocking helps us eliminate multitasking, prevent procrastination, and set ourselves up to succeed.

HOW TO DO IT

Create a to-do list, then block off time in your schedule for each specific task. Consult the sidebar "Prioritize Like a Pro" (see page 72) for support in determining the best time to complete challenging or high-priority tasks and easy or low-priority tasks. Mark the tasks in a calendar or day planner so you know when you're working on what. If you don't have enough time to complete the task within the time block, allow that information to help you regroup and course correct for next time.

#30 *When in Doubt, Write It Out!*

WHY IT WORKS

When the going gets tough, the tough get . . . writing? According to author, entrepreneur, and motivational speaker Jim Rohn, "If you're serious about becoming a wealthy, powerful, sophisticated, healthy, influential, cultured, and unique individual, keep a journal."

All right, Jim, what if we're just trying to keep our closet organized?

No matter the motivation, journaling appears to be much more than "Dear diary, today my crush borrowed my pencil!" It boasts incredible scientific benefits such as decreased stress, increased clarity, heightened self-awareness, enhanced problem-solving abilities, decreased anxiety/depression, better-quality sleep, increased positive mood/affect, and even improved memory. *Like a one-stop feel-good shop!*

Reason being: The act of writing taps into that rational, analytical *left side* of the brain while simultaneously freeing up the *right side* to get creative, playful, and intuitive—making journaling extra powerful.

Lesson learned? When in doubt, put pen to paper! Effective journaling occurs daily for 10 to 15 minutes, ideally. For tips on how to do this, we turn to the Center for Journal Therapy, which offers this helpful acronym for beginning: WRITE.

HOW TO DO IT

W: What. What have your thoughts been about lately? Write down what's happening in your life.

R: Review or reflect. Reflect on what's been going on. Ease into it with some deep breathing or meditation. How does *W* make you feel?

I: Investigate. Investigate your feelings or thoughts and keep writing. Refocus if you get stuck.

T: Time yourself. Write your journaling start and anticipated stop time at the top of the page. Set a timer to buzz at your goal writing time.

E: Exit smart. Read what you've written and reflect in a few sentences. Note any action steps.

Prioritize Like a Pro

A lengthy to-do list can be overwhelming, especially if we don't have a plan for how to tackle it. More so if our boss gives us one more big to-do, due tomorrow! How do we alleviate the pressure and begin to organize? And how do we know *when* to prioritize *what*?

This chart can help. Eisenhower's decision matrix (yes, designed by that Eisenhower) helps us organize tasks by importance and urgency. Important tasks contribute to goal achievement, whereas urgent tasks require immediate attention.

Quadrant 1 is for deadline-driven projects or crises.

Quadrant 2 is for planning or strategizing.

Quadrant 3 is for urgent but unimportant tasks like interruptions requiring immediate attention.

Quadrant 4 is for time wasters.

Use this chart to help you organize to-dos accordingly, with a critical eye on whether your tasks are focused on bringing you closer to your goal. The objective is to spend most of our time in quadrant 2.

Eisenhower Decision Matrix

	URGENT	NOT URGENT
IMPORTANT	**1** • crises • emergencies • pressing problems • deadline-driven projects • last minute-preparations	**2** • preparations, planning, prevention • capability improvement • relationship building • true recreation/relaxation
NOT IMPORTANT	**3** • interruptions • some calls/emails • some meetings • some pressing matters • popular activities	**4** • busy work • trivial activities • some calls/emails • escape activities • time wasters

#31 *Cultivate Compassion*

WHY IT WORKS

If we find it difficult to accomplish something we believe is supposed to be easy—from, let's say, being on time more often to curbing our spending—we may, understandably, become frustrated. If a particular task that supposedly shouldn't be that hard proves more difficult than we imagined, we're left feeling discouraged. When this occurs for my clients, I'll encourage them to break down goals into bite-size chunks so that they can start by successfully accomplishing one small part of the task. Yet, if they believe they *should* be able to do the whole thing at once, going step-by-step may feel silly, or ridiculous even.

It's a lose-lose recipe that halts progress and leads to defeat. But adding one key ingredient can help us start to win, and that's *compassion*. It's a word many have come to associate with going easy on ourselves or simply accepting where we're at. Yet here's something interesting . . .

"Most people have gotten it wrong because our culture says being hard on yourself is the way to be," says Dr. Kristin Neff, a pioneer in self-compassion research. She says most people believe the less compassion they give to themselves, the better they can stick to their goals. "Although they believe self-criticism is what keeps them in line, in truth . . . self-compassion is really conducive to motivation."

In her book *The Willpower Instinct*, health psychologist Kelly McGonigal agrees, writing that study after study "shows that self-criticism is consistently associated with less motivation and worse self-control. Surprisingly, it's forgiveness, not guilt, that increases accountability."

Yep! Compassion, forgiveness, all those things our mama taught us to do for others actually *really* help us, too.

And—for the real clincher!—the people who find it the easiest to be supportive and understanding with others often (surprisingly) score the lowest on self-compassion tests, berating themselves for perceived failures like being overweight or not exercising. *Where's the karma, I ask you!*

Now that we understand this tendency, let's aim to remedy it.

HOW TO DO IT

1. **Identify areas where it feels easier to be critical rather than compassionate with yourself and vice versa.** And remember, *it's all okay*. We're simply observing, getting a lay of the land so we can begin creating change.

2. **Decide what self-compassion might look like for you.** Is it leaving yourself a little note in the morning saying, "I'm doing great"? Is it practicing more forgiveness toward yourself? How?

3. **Implement it.** Implementing this might feel totally silly or awkward at first. Yet, the more you try this strategy, the easier it will become. And beyond priming you for success, these practices will—simply put—help you feel better, too.

#32 Have a Strategy in the First Place

WHY IT WORKS

If you've found a strategy that resonates with you, that you're willing to try out, let alone implement, let alone *keep implementing*, consider yourself ahead of the game! Because it can feel so much easier to *wait* to buy the book. To wait to read it. To slip it into our bookshelf and instead opt to maintain some general awareness or hazy sense of how we'll actually meet our goals. Like "I'll just remember I'm not going to procrastinate when it's a gorgeous day out and the beach is five minutes away" or "when it's a rainy day out and the newest season of my favorite show just dropped on Netflix."

As a go-with-the-flow type of gal myself, I know simply bearing a goal in mind might deceptively *feel* easiest. But if we don't use tools to take action toward our goal, we won't be able to enjoy the process of getting there and seeing our goal come to fruition.

Instead, by having a strategy, implementing it, and knowing how we'll act when that forbidden fruit is passed our way, we increase our chance of success.

HOW TO DO IT

1. **Pick a strategy or two that you vibe with.** The strategies should feel doable or make sense to you.

2. **Write it down and earmark the page it's on.** Think about it.

3. **Implement it.** When you want to switch things up, just try out another.

#33 *Moderation over Deprivation*

WHY IT WORKS

When you set out to achieve your willpower goal, did you think to yourself, "I really hope this takes a while so I can be challenged for the next year and struggle to resist temptation after temptation, again and again. Pretty please?" Likely not. For most of us, it's more like "Direct me to the nearest easy button, thank you!" However, we're usually not the push of a button or a magic spell away from attaining our desires. And when that truth sinks in, it's easy to become disappointed and left craving some sort of quick solution. Something to help us achieve our goal faster or at least put off that painful reality that good things take a little time. Ironically, the quick fix we might somehow stumble upon is often the exact habit we want to move away from: "Wait, you mean to tell me I might not be able to stop smoking in under a week? Jeez. *I need a cigarette!*"

If we don't turn to our old vices in an effort to calm our nerves, we may try creating a different easy button. Using a stimulant to get that assignment done. Overexercising or implementing a similarly strict, unsustainable action plan in an attempt to fast-track success. These shortcuts, beyond bordering on dangerous, actually create much more work for us in the long run. Instead of banking on our ability to transform and/or even enjoy the growth process, we're banking on a Band-Aid solution. We're Band-Aiding the symptom—smoking, overeating, overspending—as opposed to moving directly and effectively toward our willpower goal.

What if we didn't see our goal and the fact that we're not there yet as an issue we had to "cover up"? What if we saw it as a process of unfolding, where we get to learn, grow, and actually become more of ourselves? How might that change our perception of the journey toward goal attainment?

To that end, let's view moderation (as opposed to deprivation or extremism) as the ideal. Yes, that means getting comfortable with the idea that we won't always get it right. That we'll order the steak, raise our voice with our kids, and maybe sneak a smoke at times. But every time we *try*, we're strengthening our willpower muscle, prioritizing our goals, and committing to our belief that we can, indeed, achieve.

HOW TO DO IT

1. **Find sustainability.** How do you eat an elephant? One bite at a time. In other words, when it comes to our goal and practicing moderation, let's move forward in a way that's actually sustainable. Instead of saying, "I can never overspend again," for example, simply work toward curbing and monitoring your spending. Limit your shopping to one day instead of several days a week, for instance, and purchase one item instead of several items. Make a list so you know exactly what you're purchasing. This way, you can measure your progress by determining whether you've stuck to or strayed from that list. You can even create a reward for yourself (see strategy #44, page 98). "If I don't shop Monday through Thursday, I'll make plans to have coffee with a friend."

2. **Focus on the process.** To increase your probability of success, make the process more interesting (see strategy #17, page 48) and important (see strategy #9, page 37) than the actual goal at hand.

#34 Find Your Flow

WHY IT WORKS

In strategy #33 (see page 77), we learned there's no such thing as an easy button. *Psst! You! Yeah, you!* Come in a little closer so I can share a secret. There is one covert workaround, a way to feel so focused, so engaged, that even the most challenging of tasks—solving for pi, reasoning with your teenager—becomes, dare I say it, *effortless!* If you're ready to embrace ease and become alert and concentrated, let go of force and instead find your flow.

You know those days that fly by, when you start in on a project—painting the living room or practicing guitar—then suddenly realize it's 6:00 p.m. and you forgot to eat lunch and misplaced your phone. Minus the hunger pangs and missed calls, you feel awesome and accomplished because you, my friend, have been in flow! Flow is that feeling of lightness, effortlessness, being in the zone—when morning turns to evening in a snap and you've spent the day (or a chunk of time) feeling fully focused and completely immersed in the task at hand.

Scientifically speaking, flow refers to effortless concentration and enjoyment, and it occurs, according to a 2010 study published in *Emotion*, through "interaction between positive affect and high attention." This almost magical state of mind is sometimes dubbed an "optimal experience," and once we experience it, we'll likely understand why. When in flow, tasks that once required effort now feel easy; experiences that might call for force or discipline now feel enjoyable. Not to mention that when we're in flow and feeling our best, we may simultaneously be doing our best, too. For example, the 2010 study found that when professional pianists give an "expert performance," they are usually in a flow state. Meaning performing at our peak may entail being fully immersed and fully in flow.

HOW TO DO IT

1. **Get (intrinsically) motivated.** In his article "The Concept of Flow," psychologist Mihaly Csikszentmihalyi says flow state is the "highest intrinsic motivation," explaining that during flow, "self-consciousness is lost, one surrenders completely to the moment, and time means nothing." When in flow state, he adds, "the individual operates at full capacity." To jump-start motivation, connect to your core values (see strategy #43, page 96) and flow from the inside out.

2. **Team up.** In 2008, three studies regarding flow state found that it's better to flow with others than flow alone. Levels of joy, satisfaction, and enjoyment were shown to be stronger when flowing with friends versus flowing in solitude. Buddy up, go to a shared workspace, and get in the zone.

3. **Make it *just* challenging enough.** To be in flow, the task needs to be challenging enough, but not too challenging. Try out tasks that meet that criteria and see what gets you in the zone (see the sidebar "How Will I Know If I'm in Flow?" page 83).

#35 Develop Routines and Rituals

WHY IT WORKS

Have you ever played Whac-A-Mole? It's this arcade game where toy moles pop up unexpectedly. Players use a mallet to give these bouncy rodents a righteous whack so they'll retreat back into their respective holes.

My two cents? The reason we humans enjoy "mole-whacking" is the instant gratification it gives us. It's fun to brace and anticipate where that next mole might come from.

In the light of day, outside the arcade, unless we want to wind up behind bars, we can't use a mallet to smack every challenge out of our way. Nor can we brace for every obstacle: our kid's after-school meltdown, our boss's disappointment in our work.

But by planning for what we can expect—and making room for what's "out-of-the-ordinary"—we can prepare. This way, we'll be ready to knock our willpower habit out of the park, even when life gets a little squirrelly.

We can do this by implementing routines and rituals. A routine is a sequence of actions that we engage in regularly—getting up, brushing our teeth, or reading the newspaper—whereas rituals typically have some sort of meaning behind them. A ritual is a routine like taking a midday walk or saying a prayer before bed, yet it feels more significant because we associate it with a positive connotation or deeper purpose.

In his book *Daily Rituals*, Mason Currey writes, "A solid routine fosters a well-worn groove for one's mental energies and helps stave off the tyranny of moods."

Meaning, when we have something to do at a certain time and in a certain way, we're more likely to be energetically prepared for it. Because it's been planned, it's less likely that an unexpected circumstance or change in mood will throw us off course.

HOW TO DO IT

1. **Know thyself.** Write down a list of the things that make you feel good. Connecting with a friend. Walking your dog while listening to your favorite podcast. After identifying your needs, you can move to step 2.

2. **Prioritize your needs.** First determine what's most important to you. Try ranking your needs on a scale from 1 to 10, 10 being most important, like you can't live without it, and 1 being not very important, at least for right now. Choose one of your higher-ranked needs to create a routine or ritual around. Let's say one of your top needs is drawing. By creating a schedule for when you will draw, you'll alleviate uncertainty around when you'll next put pen to paper and have a plan for when and how you'll do it.

3. **Try it out.** Try out your new routine or ritual for a week and track what happens. Was it easy to stick to? Did you get off track? If so, ask yourself, "What can I do to minimize veering off course next time?" Gather information and use it to inform your next steps.

How Will I Know If I'm in Flow?

Flow: that mecca we all want to experience, where previously difficult tasks suddenly seem exciting and doable. How can we achieve flow? Psychologist Mihaly Csikszentmihalyi identifies a number of subjective criteria for being in a flow state, or fully immersed in the moment and activity at hand. These include a sense or experience of:

Full concentration in the present moment

The merging of action and awareness

The loss of self-awareness

The ability to control your actions and deal with situations because you know what comes next

Time flying

The activity as intrinsically rewarding, that the goal is an excuse for the process

When you realize you've met those criteria, consider yourself at your most focused and naturally determined, so keep going with that flow! (See strategy #34, page 79.)

#36 Expand Your Self-Awareness

WHY IT WORKS

Did you know that we spend 50 percent of our time on autopilot, meaning 50 percent of the time our mind wanders from the task at hand? In other words, 50 percent of the time we're grocery shopping, listening to our sister's story about her coworkers, or doing the dishes, we're actually ruminating about our client, thinking about what's for dinner, or trying to recall that funny joke from our favorite TV show. If we're only ever *really* here half the time, it's understandable that half the time we might slip up on our willpower habit—be quick to anger or eat the brownies. Although we may physically be there, if we're not mentally present, our choices—most likely—might be mindless.

So, how do we increase our awareness and make more thoughtful, constructive, in-the-moment choices, ones that reflect our long-term goals? The key is to become more self-aware. By focusing on what we have going on inside—our "internal states, preference, resources, and intuitions," as defined by Daniel Goleman, author of *Emotional Intelligence*—we're able to make better decisions regarding the goings-on around us. The more present we become to our temptations, impulses, inclinations, and responses, the more we can actively create positive change.

Besides simply making better decisions, if we're experiencing ego depletion, self-awareness can act like a personal "power up"—for all my video gamers, think the super mushroom to our Mario or the power pellet to our Pac-Man or, simply, a boost—helping us maintain self-control even after we've already exerted willpower on another task.

I am the way I am. Or am I? We have much more control over the way we think, feel, and behave than we tend to realize. If you aren't bowled over by certain results you see in your life, practice observing—instead of engaging in—your thoughts. In other words, don't believe everything you think! To begin, check out the following three-step formula.

HOW TO DO IT

1. **Be your own observer.** Observe the way you typically think or behave in similar situations.

2. **Get curious.** Why might I be having that thought? Refrain from judgment and drop into wonder.

3. **Decide.** Is this thought good for me? Even if it feels true, what alternate *positive* possibilities can I focus on here?

#37 Temptation-Proof Your Environment

WHY IT WORKS

"When a flower doesn't bloom, you fix the environment in which it grows, not the flower," says inspirational speaker Alexander den Heijer. How relieving is that? If the key to increased willpower was less *look inside* and more *fix the outside*, you could simply prune the pastries from your pantry and weed out the waffles. Instead of mastering a whole new self-control strategy, simply "water" what's working and cut out what's not.

In a *Business Insider* interview, Duke University psychologist Dan Ariely says, "Environment matters. We think that we make decisions on our own, but the environment influences us to a great degree. Because of that, we need to think about how to change our environment."

If we didn't have Candy Crush Saga on our phone, we wouldn't have to resist playing it. If we didn't have Netflix on our TV, we'd be far less tempted to watch it. Big ask, I know! But when we eliminate what's enticing, we create freedom from its grip. Meaning no more "should I or shouldn't I." No more wondering whether you'll play it, watch it, eat it. No more mulling the options and being stuck in indecision.

By removing the video games or the donuts from our living room, our cabinet, or our line of vision, the choice has been made for us. When it comes to triggers in our apartment or office, we're now, quite literally, home free.

HOW TO DO IT

1. **Identify temptations.** What in your environment isn't conducive to achieving your goals? A bowl of M&Ms on the kitchen countertop? News alert notifications on your computer?

2. **Remove, replace, or reschedule temptations.** If you'd like to curb mindless snacking, gaming, or other indulging and remain focused while working, simply remove, replace, or reorganize these barriers to success. Notice how we don't always have to get rid of them. Instead of tossing out the candy bowl, we can add fruit to it! If removing notifications altogether seems too big a jump, we can start by rescheduling our phone's news alert settings to only go off when we have a scheduled break.

3. **Remember to moderate your expectations.** Reaching for those M&Ms and feeling an apple instead may initially be a shock to the system! Remind yourself why the apples are there and refresh yourself on your long-term goal. Soon enough you'll become acclimated to a temptation-free environment, and soon enough you'll find a sense of peace in it. And that alone may just be the perfect treat.

#38 Steer toward Success

WHY IT WORKS

In her book *A Return to Love*, Marianne Williamson writes, "Our deepest fear is not that we are inadequate. Our deepest fear is that we are powerful beyond measure. It is our light, not our darkness, that most frightens us."

Imagine it's never been about not being good enough, failing, or the possibility that we'd give up. It's *never been* about lacking the confidence, intelligence, or some innate ability to achieve.

If we've experienced nervousness about committing to our goal, what if it's *never been* because we're worried we'll fail, but the total opposite? What if, deep down, the apprehension is about *our ability*—our brilliance, our light, our talent, our strength—and what would actually happen if we brought all of it to the table?

Who would we be if *we succeeded*?

What if we've only ever seen ourselves as someone who hasn't quite lived up to their potential? Someone who hasn't quite been able to get healthy, be in a satisfying relationship, or make more money. Who would we be if we did? Would we still be liked? Would our friends and family still support us?

These questions may seem silly, but if we think about them, they make complete sense. If we've always been the person who is liked for being agreeable and compliant, then if we vocalize our true feelings more often, this might inevitably impact the dynamics of our relationships. If we've never felt capable of earning a solid income, where does that deep-rooted identity of consistently feeling financially unstable go when we start to earn? And *can* we actually earn if we're holding on to that feeling?

If our desire to succeed is strong, but we're simultaneously, perhaps subconsciously, fearing the consequences of that success, then even if we put our best foot forward, these subconscious beliefs can undermine us.

We may, perhaps subconsciously, *avoid* instead of *welcome* positive opportunities. Not accept the salsa dancing date when asked. Not put our all into our workout. Not grasp an opportunity to succeed so we can keep ourselves safely at homeostasis—and thus continue to be with what we know.

Let's change that, all right? Because we can dance if we want to. And we may not have to leave our friends behind.

HOW TO DO IT

1. **Instead of fearing the loss, embrace the gain.** Picture the endless possibilities that using your resources and endeavoring to attain success will grant you. More time. More energy. More abundance. More freedom. More connection. More self-trust. More fulfillment.

2. **Determine where you're making fear- versus excitement-based choices.** Fear-based choices are ones made out of worry or feeling like you *have* to, or *else*. Excitement-based choices are decisions that come from feeling eager, like you *want* to.

#39 Connect with Community

WHY IT WORKS

While writing this book with a fast-approaching deadline, I figured, "Better lock myself away to stay on track!" I canceled plans. Hammered a skull-and-crossbones Do Not Enter sign on my office door. Okay, I didn't go *that* far, but in an effort to buckle down and finish this book, I actually encountered a little problem: I sometimes felt alone and uninspired. This was hardly the perfect recipe for churning out vibrant creative writing.

Here's something remarkable and somewhat obvious: If we want to spike our own levels of motivation, just be around others who are motivated. (Oh. *Duh!*) But here's what's not so obvious—it's not just *any* others; it's people we *believe* are intrinsically motivated (see strategy #43, page 96). We can sense that passion, not some pot of gold at the end of the rainbow, is what drives them to persevere.

In a 2010 study on social contagion of motivation, students reported that their own intrinsic motivation to engage in a certain activity was influenced by their view of their teacher's intrinsic motivation.

In other words, if I'm sitting next to you and I think you're motivated by your own volition, I'm going to be more motivated. Furthermore, if I'm surrounded by motivated, inquisitive, and participative people, my environment becomes this enhanced breeding ground for engagement and empowerment—even one where I perform better.

HOW TO DO IT

Brainstorm people you know who are passionate. These are people who are consistently engaged in various projects and/or working on things. Ask them to point you to a group, a club, a book club, or a virtual or in-person meetup for people with shared goals. Join a shared workspace!

#40 Recognize Your Reaction

WHY IT WORKS

I had a client, who I'll call Jessica, who wanted to create online marketing videos. Every time she went to film, though, she became nervous and thought, "Do I look okay?" and "Will my message come across?" These thoughts were totally understandable! However, her reaction turned what might have been a 30-minute-long project into an hour of debating, changing outfits, and rethinking messaging.

Instead of denying or pushing away Jessica's apprehensions, together we planned for them. We set aside 10 minutes for her to journal her concerns, letting them out by writing them down. Afterward, Jessica reported feeling lighter, ready to record.

It's easy to brush off or pretend we don't have the reactions or feelings we do. But in doing so, we're denying a part of us that wants to be nurtured. As a result of recognizing and not minimizing Jessica's concerns around filming, making space for all her thoughts, the nervous feelings and reactions lessened over time. By addressing these feelings before filming, she could act in spite of them. Soon enough, she no longer needed to journal and could just press record.

HOW TO DO IT

Seek insight. Instead of seeing triggers as the enemy, see them as a clue—an insight into the mystery of how we work and why we work that way. As opposed to thinking, "I cave under pressure," try thinking, "I wonder why perceived pressure makes me feel stressed?" How can you view pressure in a way that allows you to feel neutral or even inspired? This may mean viewing pressure as an *opportunity*. Whether or not you thrive, you get to experience something cool and learn from your experience.

Expand Your Consciousness

Not to sound totally New Age or "woo," but when we're endeavoring to start down a new path—quitting a strong habit or developing boundaries in our relationships—having a more expansive perspective can support us tremendously. This means not seeing the problem the same way we've always seen it—"I can't stop procrastinating!" or "I can't quit spending!"—but choosing to view it through a different, clearer lens. Because when you change the way you look at things, the things you look at change.

To start, ask yourself empowering questions, remember the things that are going well, and remain solution oriented instead of focusing on blocks or problems. Consider the following questions if you're feeling stuck:

When have I persisted in the past despite doubt?

How can I stay the course even though I'm experiencing an impulse to stray from my willpower habit?

If I were advising a friend who was experiencing the same challenge, what might I tell them?

#41 Build New Habits

WHY IT WORKS

In his book *The Power of Habit: Why We Do What We Do in Life and Business,* author Charles Duhigg writes, "Any behavior that can be reduced to a routine is one less behavior that we must spend time and energy consciously thinking about and deciding upon."

Imagine *that*. What feels unnatural or unattainable in the here and now—tracking your spending or consistently keeping a clean home—could be second nature, as easy as walking or tying a shoe.

The key is simply to try that new, potentially challenging activity or habit, then keep trying it again and again. Let go of any doubt around succeeding and instead emphasize consistent effort. Remember to pick up the book instead of the remote. Hit the stop button instead of snooze. After two months of actively reminding yourself to do these things, you'll no longer have to remember.

You'll just be that avid reader or early riser—someone who committed to keep going and to keep trying. That's all you need to do.

HOW TO DO IT

1. **Start slow**. Let's take the pressure off, okay? You're doing this because it's something you want to do, not something you have to do perfectly.

2. **Commit to trying.** You don't have to commit to succeeding. Just commit to trying. When you watch TV instead of reading, try again. When you snooze instead of starting your day, circle back tomorrow.

3. **Stay consistent.** If you do these things in the same context— around the same time—eventually they'll become automated, meaning less thinking, just being.

#42 See Stress through a New Lens

WHY IT WORKS

Imagine that when overwhelming feelings and pressure show up at work or home, instead of pushing these emotions away or getting aggravated by their arrival, we accepted—even invited—this stress into our lives. Considering all we see on the news reiterates stress's link to multiple adverse health effects, the idea of welcoming stress with open arms is a strange one.

But what if it weren't the stress itself creating these conditions we hear about—from disease to stroke to even heart attack—but the way we've been taught to view stress? According to a 2012 study, simply *perceiving* stress as negative is correlated with poor physical and mental health, along with a higher risk of pre-mature death.

Now, don't let that fact stress you out. Or do, but consider that stress as natural, or perhaps positive! According to health psychologist Kelly McGonigal, the harmful effects of stress on health "are not inevitable," and how you "think about stress" and "how you act can transform your experience of stress." When you choose to view your stress response as helpful, you "create the biology of courage."

HOW TO DO IT

Take a moment to accept stress. The next time experiencing stress triggers negative thoughts for you, pause and consider what it might be like to just get on board with those more pressured feelings. What might accepting the stress as a normal, inevitable, and even beneficial part of endeavoring to reach your goal be like? Perhaps strange at first! But if accepting stress was truly an opportunity to create more courage, how would that change your thoughts around letting it in?

#43 Identify Intrinsic Motivators

WHY IT WORKS

Imagine if we only chose goals based on what we're told we're good at, what our friends or colleagues strive for, or what we believe is cool or the path of least resistance. Imagine we set our sights on building a million-dollar business, when in reality sharing knowledge and creating value and connection within a nonprofit is what would truly fulfill us—or vice versa.

Extrinsic goals such as getting the promotion, landing a lead role, or taking that dream vacation can be enticing. Yet, if we find ourselves lacking motivation or feeling unfulfilled on our journey toward these alluring objectives, we can become confused, doubtful, or unsatisfied.

This disconnect may have less to do with our actual drive or self-confidence, though, and more to do with understanding what *truly* motivates us.

By learning to identify your intrinsic motivators, or the values that matter most to you—such as connection, peace, freedom, fun, achievement, prestige, family, or the like—you can more easily recognize and pursue what will actually fulfill you. And when we direct our energy toward what motivates us most, passion, excitement, and forward momentum become natural by-products.

HOW TO DO IT

1. **Select your top five intrinsic motivators.** There are no wrong answers here—everyone is different. Your most authentic motivators might be different from whatever drives your friends and family, and that's okay! The most important thing is that your answers resonate with *you*.

Feel free to choose from the list below, or come up with your own.

1. Abundance
2. Acceptance
3. Achievement
4. Contribution
5. Curiosity
6. Family
7. Freedom
8. Fun
9. Health
10. Humor
11. Leadership
12. Loyalty
13. Motivation
14. Passion
15. Professionalism
16. Responsibility
17. Stability
18. Trustworthiness
19. Understanding
20. Warmth

2. **Decide how you can incorporate more of those motivators as you progress toward your goal.** How can you experience, for example, more *freedom* at home? Or *connection* at work?

3. **Keep your motivators top of mind.** Write them down and pin them to your bulletin board or add them as a phone background, so when opportunities arise, you'll know how to choose what's most important to you.

#44 Experiment with Extrinsic Motivators

WHY IT WORKS

In the previous strategy, we explored extrinsic and intrinsic motivators. If fulfillment and passionate pursuit of our dreams require intrinsic motivation, are extrinsic motivators, such as hitting our income goal or treating ourselves to a spa day, irrelevant?

I guess we could say it depends. Not all extrinsic motivators are created equal. And they vary from person to person. Praise and recognition, for example, are proven to be highly effective extrinsic motivators—perhaps even more than money! In their book *The Carrot Principle*, authors Adrian Gostick and Chester Elton found that when organizations recognized the good work of their employees, return on equity was three times higher.

So, should our BFF high-five us whenever we forgo that post-dinner cigarette? Or, maybe we tell our boss that a smiley face sticker on our quarterly review would really go a long way. Or, perhaps the carrot we seek is a manicure if we go seven days without biting our nails. Or, a steak dinner if we go a month without eating red meat.

HOW TO DO IT

Decide on a reward and see whether implementing it impacts you. Here is a perfect opportunity to invite some experimentation into your willpower habit as you progress. Try out a few enticing ideas—putting money into your vacation account or getting a massage for hitting your willpower goals. If you find that having a reward helps you move forward, or you're successful in achieving the reward, keep doing it! Think of it like a personal science experiment—testing (and tracking!) what works best for you.

#45 Strengthen Your Self-Control

WHY IT WORKS

How might your life change if you loved *practicing*—doing something again and again, becoming better and better at it? What if you treasured opportunities to exert self-control and got excited about embracing the discomfort that comes with trying?

This might sound completely backward, but imagine we decided that instead of being implausible, or never-ending, this building willpower thing was an adventure? *Your* adventure. Your very own journey you get to embark on, be imperfect on, love up on—and you may even learn to enjoy the ride.

Here's why practice makes *progress* and why that is what we're aiming for.

Remember ego depletion, the theory that after we exert self-control it's harder to do so again? On the flip side, the same way muscles become stronger with exercise, exerting self-control regularly improves willpower strength.

Meaning the more willpower you use, the more willpower you (ultimately) gain. And we don't have to limit exerting self-control exclusively to a specific activity, either. Professor and author Cal Newport, who writes about digital tech, culture, and how the two inhibit and support our work, took a close look at the research of Roy Baumeister and others who have studied willpower. "Introducing a small number of targeted, regular self-control activities in your daily routine—such as 'spending money or exercise,'" he summarizes in a 2008 web post, "can generate improvements in unrelated areas such as 'studying and household chores.'"

HOW TO DO IT

1. **Make it fun!** Give yourself a mini challenge. Identify five to 10 areas where you can practice willpower or self-discipline.

2. **Practice exerting discipline.** One thing my clients like to do is to try on the word *discipline*. What does it feel like in your body? When you think of discipline, who comes to mind? How do they act or behave when they need to get something done? How do you think they feel? Imagine putting on a discipline hat and see what comes up for you.

3. **Reward yourself.** Give yourself "points" when you're able to resist an impulse. Save a spreadsheet on your phone that tracks all the times you successfully resist an urge.

Case Study: To Date or Not to Date

One of my clients felt satisfied in her friendships and career but felt she *should* start dating because she *should* aim to find a long-term partner. When she realized her motivation was coming from this place of should, she began to question whether she actually wanted it. "Is dating just checking a box in the 'I did this' list of life boxes we're encouraged to check?" she wondered.

To determine whether dating was truly important to her, we looked to her intrinsic motivators (see strategy #43, page 96), which we found were intimacy, connection, and companionship. When she recognized her desire to get those things met—the values that mattered most *to her*—it finally clicked. She did want to date!

It wasn't because she *should* want to "get married," for example (a thought that left her with little motivation to "put herself out there"). By identifying her specific motivation—experiencing closeness—she was able to generate the willpower to get that need met because it mattered to her.

#46 *Think Positive*

WHY IT WORKS

Theodore Roosevelt is often quoted as saying, "Believe you can, and you're halfway there." A very inspirational thought! Let's break this down for a second. If merely "believing" actually got us 50 percent closer to our goal, our total time spent would be cut in half by simply choosing to put faith in positive possibility. We'd already be 50 percent closer to never lighting another cigarette, 50 percent closer to remaining calm during heated arguments, and 50 percent closer to never biting our nails again. Now, I don't know about you, but if I could make it halfway to my goal by just deciding to believe in myself? Well, practicing that self-belief would be the very first thing I'd do.

Now, there may not be any official data demonstrating that believing in the possibility of success brings us exactly 50 percent closer to it, but there is overwhelming evidence that having a growth mindset—thinking positive and believing you can—brings us far.

Martin Seligman, a psychologist and leading figure in the field of positive psychology, writes in the *Harvard Business Review* that "people who don't give up have a habit of interpreting setbacks as temporary, local and changeable." When these people encounter something difficult, they think to themselves, "I can get through this" as opposed to "Time to throw in the towel."

Take it from the US Army, of all places. They implemented a resilience-building training for drill sergeants that actually prioritizes being optimistic. The main premise of the training is that *mental toughness comes from thinking like an optimist.* Yep! Replace "bite the bullet" with "think happy thoughts." On the double, that is . . .

In the program, drill sergeants learn to reflect on their beliefs around failure, noting whether they feel like they don't have control over the outcome and the effects are forever, or whether it's temporary and they can move forward and ultimately succeed.

In order to *think* happy, you don't always have to *be* happy. But prioritizing your own happiness in order to reach your goals and make life all-around better seems like a pretty cool formula for success.

HOW TO DO IT

1. **Don't sweat the small stuff.** It's easy to agonize over the tiniest things that in the moment feel incredibly warranted: "Yes, the toilet paper should obviously pull from the top!" Instead, choose to let go of what you can and save your time and energy for things that really matter. Focus on the big picture.

2. **Find the good.** If we're given 10 compliments and one criticism, guess which one we're more likely to remember? Hint: It's not the one that makes us blush! When experiencing negativity bias, our brain's inclination is to focus on the negative. Recognize when you're labeling something as "bad" or giving the negative more attention than the neutral or good.

#47 Let Your Progress Inform Your Process

WHY IT WORKS

In tai chi, the Chinese martial art, there's this philosophy: If an opponent is coming toward you, instead of defending or fighting against them, go with the flow of their movement. This way, you don't have to exert extra energy in pushing back or stopping them. Because interestingly enough, using force to resist force leaves both sides primed for injury.

Now, whether you're seeking to strengthen your tai chi game or are in the 95 percent of readers looking to improve a different willpower habit, there's so much we can learn from this tactic. Instead of butting against whatever challenge you may face on your willpower journey, put down your dukes and embrace it. You heard me—snuggle up and get all cozy with it! Because that obstacle doesn't necessarily have to be an annoyance or block. In reality, it's potentially an *opportunity* to help us understand ourselves better: our knee-jerk reactions, what we'll do in the face of temptation or stress, or how we'll respond when things do or don't go our way.

Instead of attacking our challenges head on, by embracing them—becoming curious about and learning from them—we can actually use them to our advantage to help inform our next steps. In other words, instead of banging your head against a wall, learn why the wall's been built in the first place. Then find a door or window to help get you to the other side.

We all have stress. Different levels of stress, different stress triggers, and different reactions to stress. Whether my clients report experiencing exorbitant or manageable amounts of stress, it's not about the *quantity* as much as it is about the *reaction*.

HOW TO DO IT

1. **Track your stress triggers.** What triggers stress for you? A looming project deadline? Snoozing five times past your alarm, then having to race to work? Making pressured decisions around what you'll order at a client lunch? Try tracking what, when, where, and how stress enters your life. Write it down in your journal.

2. **Track your reactions and coping mechanisms.** Become acutely aware of *how you react* when you experience this stress. Do you shop? Eat? Yell? Isolate? Smoke? Talk it out with a friend? Problem-solve? Help others? The next time you feel anxious or pressured, imagine pausing, then rewinding time and pinpointing what triggered that stress—almost like you're watching a replay in a football game. By observing it in slo-mo, we can gain a superior understanding of what really happened when we felt stress because we were "running late to work" or had to "make a quick decision." Remember, there's no right or wrong here. The name of the game isn't "judging our moves"—it's gaining insight into how to improve them.

3. **Let your progress inform your process.** Understanding how we progress through stress can help inform our process for avoiding, alleviating, and coping with stress moving forward. By monitoring and shifting, we can react in a way that serves us, others, and perhaps even lives we don't directly touch.

#48 Two Steps Forward, Two Steps Back?

WHY IT WORKS

Let's say your willpower habit is going along swimmingly. You're making tons of progress, taking two steps forward and one step back, but either way, dancing into some uncharted territory— forward momentum! Even your friends take notice. Your BFF congratulates you on all the strides you've made toward, let's say, giving up smoking. You feel good—*so* good, in fact, that you find yourself purchasing a pack of cigarettes to celebrate.

Why might we do this? Realize we're succeeding, then reward ourselves by "letting loose" with our "former flame"?

There are these two competing desires, explains health psychologist Kelly McGonigal. The desire to stay the course and continue eating healthy, for instance, and the desire to, well, eat the dang pie. When we're continuously gratifying one of our desires, the other will become impatient, knock on our door, and shout, "Hey you! What about me?"

So, we'll open the door, satisfy the desire, smoke the cigarette, eat the pie. We've been doing well so far, so don't we deserve it?

If we find we're taking two steps forward, then two steps right on back to where we started, let's pause this little square dance. Instead of going cold turkey on our vices, by creating planned indulgences we no longer have to resort to unplanned regressions.

HOW TO DO IT

Plan to indulge. Oh, I like this strategy already! By scheduling our indulgences, we can avoid feeling like we're on this totally regimented diet. Instead, by planning how, when, and where we will "enjoy that treat," we alleviate strict limitations and create freedom in the knowing.

#49 Make Decisions from Your Visions

WHY IT WORKS

First things first, when I say "visions," I'm not talking about whipping out a crystal ball and conducting a séance. Yet, paradoxically, we *can* predict our future if we envision it in the present.

When people visualize specific events coming to fruition, studies suggest they will rate the likelihood of these events actually happening as "high." And as we know from strategy #10 (see page 38), when we expect to achieve our vision, we tend to operate from a place of positivity, confidence, and excitement.

Meaning the "achieve my dream" equation should look something like this: visualize achieving + feel happy about it = achieving!

But, here's where most of us get this process wrong. Research from the University of California finds it's not simply picturing yourself completing an ironman triathlon, for example, or marrying the woman of your dreams. It's picturing the steps, the actual process behind those achievements.

In other words, if you've been dreaming of making $100,000 this year, swap out that mental picture for one where you envision yourself doing the work required to get that raise or researching and implementing new income streams for your business.

If you've been fantasizing meeting and marrying your dream woman, replace those fantasies with going to two networking events per week, joining a book club, and going on a certain number of dates per month, and then reevaluating and course correcting.

I know. It's not the *sexiest* visualization. But now your dream actually has the greatest potential of coming true. Because, quite frankly, you planned on it.

HOW TO DO IT

1. **Use the SMART goal creation process.** That's Specific, Measurable, Achievable, Relevant, and Time-Bound goals (see page 18). Check out the goals and subgoals you've created and the path you've devised for getting from *A* to *B*.

2. **Visualize the process.** If you've been picturing having "a lean, healthy body," for example, you don't have to get rid of that visualization if it feels supportive. Simply begin to incorporate the process for achieving that goal. Before going to bed, picture yourself getting up with your alarm, putting on your sneakers, and heading to the gym. Picture yourself cooking a delicious vegetable dish and enjoying eating it. If you've encountered specific setbacks, visualize how you'll act in the face of those setbacks in the future so you can stick to your long-term goal.

#50 Momentum: Keep the Party Going!

WHY IT WORKS

Click the remote, your TV turns on. Put a dollar in the vending machine, the Starburst is yours. Tap your Facebook app icon, you're connected to friends, family, and every acquaintance you've ever met. You can move your index finger less than an inch to join your favorite characters on a show, satisfy your sweet tooth, and reunite with everyone you know and love (and a guy you sat next to on a bus once).

It's an instant-gratification kind of world, and our mind thrives on it. With our willpower habit, though, we won't necessarily hit our goal the exact second we start progressing toward it. Dearest me! What's a brain wired for instant gratification to do?

The answer? Redefine success so we can be gratified along the way. Instead of making success equal to *achieving* the goal, let's make the goal equal to *committing to the process* of getting there: being in forward momentum and taking consistent action, regardless of the outcome.

HOW TO DO IT

1. **Select an action.** Instead of focusing on the results you want, focus on the actions you want to take. Let's say you're in sales and want 10 yeses from 10 cold calls. If you make the first five and hear no, you'll want to stop if you're driven by outcomes. Instead, change your goal to simply making the 10 cold calls regardless of their outcome.

2. **Use it as an opportunity.** Whether or not the next five calls are yeses, by at least making them, you're practicing your skills and creating the opportunity for five more yeses.

Hire a Coach

A bunch of folks got a life coach, and 99 percent found it a rewarding experience, according to one study from the International Coach Federation. A whopping 96 percent said they'd do it again. Nearly two-thirds reported improvements in their work performance, and four out of every five said their confidence increased.

In a 2014 *Business Insider* article, writer Richard Feloni explores President Bill Clinton's relationship with his own coach, the renowned Tony Robbins. In a 2007 speech, Clinton shared that Robbins "not only [has] the gift to inspire, but he really, from my point of view, teaches the most important lesson that every individual has to learn about living day to day, which is that you have choices in every circumstance."

So, what exactly can a life coach help with? They'll support you in determining what success in your life looks like for you, specifically. They'll help you uncover potential blocks to fulfillment and create a safe space for you to gain clarity and go from good to great, from surviving to thriving. Professional coaches become companions in your growth, cheerleaders for your success, and accountability partners who help you remain committed to your goals.

#51 Disarm Cognitive Distortions: Part One

WHY IT WORKS

We've got support. We've got a plan. We've got a strategy—or 75! But we've also got some sneaky cognitive distortions on our plate: thought patterns that *seem* logical when in fact they're a distorted way in which we may be viewing ourselves, other people, experiences, the world. Why might our mind distort our reality? Our brain is actually trying to do us a solid, preserving whatever preconceived notions we have about ourselves, our abilities, others, and life in general—even though these ideas may be inaccurate or less than helpful. By knowing how to identify these stealthily disguised thoughts, we can learn to disarm them. Let's start with two concepts: mental filtering and magnification and minimization.

First, picture taking inventory of your willpower journey: the time you got up early and hit the gym three days in a row and the time you gave in and ate the ice cream at your neighbor's BBQ. The times you succeeded, the times you stagnated, the times you backtracked. Now imagine taking a magnifying glass and looking only at the experiences that seemed like failures. If things don't *ever* seem to be working, it's likely not because they aren't. Our mind may simply be engaging in "mental filtering," a cognitive distortion in which we focus exclusively on what's *not* working and filter what *is* working out of our conscious awareness.

Instead of getting discouraged or even attempting to "move our magnifying glass" over to the nearest puppy, rainbow, or unicorn, simply notice that tendency to narrow in on the negative in the first place. When we recognize it, we can change it!

And speaking of magnifying, when experiencing the "magnification and minimization" cognitive distortion, we may similarly discount the positive and expound upon the negative. For instance, if we gave a presentation at work and forgot to include three important slides, even if we received positive feedback, we'll focus exclusively on forgetting the slides as opposed to remembering all the accolades from our supervisor and colleagues.

HOW TO DO IT

1. **Familiarize yourself.** If we think about it scientifically, these distortions are just our brain's misguided attempts at pointing us in the right direction, so let's have some compassion for ourselves. We all engage in these from time to time. Becoming familiar with these distortions and embracing honesty leads us to step 2.

2. **Identify (and challenge!) distortions in the moment.** If it feels like everything seems to be going wrong, challenge yourself to pinpoint facts versus opinions. For instance, if we felt our presentation went terribly, the fact might be "I did a presentation," whereas the opinion might be "it didn't go well." A fact is something proven, such as "this is the letter *W*," whereas an opinion is simply one point of view about that fact, such as "that *W* would look better in a different font." To gain clarity, distinguish facts from opinions and question the truth of the situation.

3. **Believe in something new.** Okay, so you don't *have* to believe anything other than what you're currently thinking. But if your thoughts aren't serving you in an optimal way, why not try on a new thought for size? You might think something like, "I did a presentation, and it went okay. There were things I would've changed, but I noticed everyone seemed happy with it. Maybe I did better than I thought." Practice thinking new, more supportive thoughts, even if they don't quite feel factual for you yet. By reiterating them—writing them down or saying them aloud to yourself—you'll find that they'll become more and more believable over time.

#52 Disarm Cognitive Distortions: Part Two

WHY IT WORKS

Welcome back! It's part 2 of the Disarm Cognitive Distortions strategies, and we're here with more riveting news regarding your brain. Now in part 1, we learned cognitive distortions are kind of like wearing a pair of 3-D glasses, like you might at the movies or on a theme park ride. That monster truck or frightening villain reaching at you through the screen seems so real. But remove your glasses and poof! It's merely a cluster of moving images hardly out to get you.

If, metaphorically speaking, we're used to living with these glasses on, it's tough to imagine we haven't always been seeing 20/20. But if particular experiences or people in your life seem to be a recurring source of frustration, try removing your "glasses" and rethinking your thoughts.

Considering we have between 50,000 and 70,000 thoughts per day, mathematically speaking it makes sense that, at the very least, one or two of those might be skewed, or simply unhelpful. To remedy this, let's concentrate on the thoughts that exhilarate us and learn to redirect our focus when it comes to the ones that feel menacing.

First let's consider what's called "personalization." Let's say we catch a coworker rolling her eyes, or we overhear a criticism and assume it's about us. We may be right, or we may be engaging in personalization, taking what others say or do and making it about ourselves. Remember, when we're experiencing this form of thinking, it feels completely rational. *We're* the reason the group dinner sucked, right? And *we're* the reason our daughter stayed out past her curfew. Even though we see ourselves as the cause of certain outcomes or the reason for others' actions or shifts in mood, we likely aren't, and likely no one's at fault.

Now let's consider what's called "overgeneralization," another form of skewed or unhelpful thinking. When we take one isolated event and associate it with all future events, we're engaging in overgeneralization. For example, if we hire an office assistant who doesn't perform as well at their job as we might like, we may believe that *all* assistants don't perform well at their jobs. If we have a bad time at an outdoor concert, we might assume *all* outdoor concerts aren't fun. Taking one experience or circumstance and assuming all future experiences or circumstances will be similar is relatively easy to do. But in doing so, we narrow our possibilities for future pleasure, purpose, fun, excitement, and experience.

HOW TO DO IT

1. **Prove yourself wrong.** Make a case for the opposite of what you believe to be true. I know—this feels hard to do, because our thoughts are coming from us. So! In order to get started . . .

2. **Be the observer.** Observe your thoughts. Take inventory of them instead of immediately buying into them. Then . . .

3. **Choose supportive thoughts.** How might someone else's actions be interpreted differently than how you're currently interpreting them? What alternate reasons might exist for why the waiter scowls as he brings you your order, for instance? If it's not because he dislikes you, could it be that he's having a bad day in general or that he's tired? Choose a more supportive reframe.

#53 Disarm Cognitive Distortions: Part Three

WHY IT WORKS

You've made it! It's the final installment of our cognitive distortions series, and boy, are you in for a treat. That is, if you'll let yourself have it. Because really, you shouldn't indulge in treats! If you sneak a candy bar or donut—temptations that most certainly aren't part of your healthy eating plan—you might as well crack open a beer, order a large pizza, light a cigarette, and officially consider the whole day a wash. Right?

When we're experiencing the "must/should" and/or "all or nothing" cognitive distortions, that throw-it-all-away mentality certainly *feels* accurate. Let's take a closer look.

Must/should thinking sounds like "I *should* be able to focus every time I want to study" or "I *must* not eat a single piece of Halloween candy" or "I *should* be happier." That there's a whole lot of must-ing and should-ing, which many of us experience on a regular basis! Picture, metaphorically speaking, giving yourself a stern slap on the wrist each time you fall short of these expectations—expectations that are often quite unrealistic. If and when we don't meet our own standards, we're left feeling frustrated, guilty, and even incapable. Instead of should-ing all over ourselves, let's rebel against the rules! By choosing to notice and question these self-imposed policies, we can alleviate pressure and increase our chance of success.

"All or nothing" thinking sounds like "if we stick to our healthy eating plan, we're *good*." If we don't, we're *bad*. If we break our healthy eating habit in the morning, we may as well spend the rest of the day eating sweets, carbs, and everything we've labeled "off-limits." When we're looking through the lens of the "all or nothing" cognitive distortion, these punishments fit the crime. And although we're not *actually* engaging in criminal activity, we still might metaphorically convict ourselves based on "bad" behavior. We'll consider situations either amazing or terrible and easily label ourselves as something positive or negative—a winner or a loser, perfect or a failure. Sounds like quite the tug-of-war! But, fear not: When we recognize we're engaging in "all or nothing" thinking, we can change it—dare I say—for the better.

HOW TO DO IT

1. **Recognize the times you use "must" or "should."** Try to do this even (and especially) when it seems innocent—like you're simply stating a truth: "I should be better at my job by now."

2. **Determine whether or not that belief is actually serving you.** See whether you can choose another word for "must" or "should." Some examples include "I'd like to . . .," "I want to . . .," "it would be nice if . . .," "it would be ideal if . . .," and "if I can, great; if not, I'll get to it later."

3. **Recognize shades of gray.** If you're engaging in "all or nothing" thinking—in right/wrong, good/bad, always/never, yeses/nos—start to recognize shades of gray. By loosening your grip and giving yourself some leeway, you can alleviate pressure and embrace tons of possibility.

#54 *Have a Fresh Start*

WHY IT WORKS

New Year's resolutions, the start of summer, or maybe *winter is coming*. All good reasons—the impetus even—for hopping on the elliptical, giving away old clothes, or redecorating our home office space.

But truth be told, we don't *need* a holiday, birthday, or season to finally make it happen. Instead, choose your own fresh-start moment anywhere—anytime!

Forget Presidents' Day or the Fourth of July. You get to decide on any season, reason, day, or time to start over, to begin again—and studies show there's good cause for it.

According to psychologist and MacArthur Fellow Angela Duckworth, fresh-start moments help people feel "disconnected from their past failures," which helps us attain long-term goals and elevates "our current self-image and confidence." When things feel stagnant—from your business to your relationship, like something's just *not clicking* anymore—remember you don't have to stay stuck in that muck! We can let go of the past and draw a line in the sand.

We don't have to wait until the first of January to have a fresh start.

HOW TO DO IT

1. **Pick a date and make it *special*.** Calendar it! Tell your friends about it for extra accountability (e.g., "On Saturday I'm going to start looking for new jobs!").

2. **Journal why you're looking forward to that date.** What's exciting about it? What will you do when that date comes? Be specific: Will you bring your laptop to a coffee shop from 10:30 a.m. to 4:00 p.m. and update your résumé?

3. **Create a ritual for the night before.** Maybe it's blowing out a candle to signify leaving a past habit behind.

#55 *Mind Your Mood*

WHY IT WORKS

Is the only bulletproof way to resist temptation to avoid it completely? Cross the street before passing your favorite clothing store or leave the party before cake is served? Cue deflating noise-maker . . .

While shifting locations before singing "Happy Birthday" is not always a viable option, shifting your mood might be. Research shows acts of self-regulation *may* deplete our psychological resources. Meaning? If we've already exerted the willpower to clean the house and lift the weights and then happen to find ourselves next to a delicious bottle of champagne we "shouldn't" open, not popping that cork may prove more difficult.

If you want to maintain your willpower, I've got a funny solution for you. Literally. In a 2007 study, researchers found that participants with depleted self-control who received surprise gifts or watched funny videos were better able to resist temptation later on than those who simply rested after exerting willpower. In other words, organic mood enhancers may improve your self-control.

So! Next time you're feeling drained—ready to bum a smoke or swipe your credit card for a pair of heels you were "just trying on" a minute earlier—pull up that funny YouTube video or watch a Jim Carrey movie instead and elevate your willpower by elevating your mood.

HOW TO DO IT

Create a list of 10 things that make you laugh or smile. It could be as simple as listening to a funny podcast or touching base with a friend. Keep your list handy, so whenever you're feeling low on willpower and need a positive boost, you're prepared.

The Power of a Note

Positive psychology expert Shawn Achor and his colleagues had employees at Facebook, Microsoft, and US Foods write a two-minute e-mail each morning thanking or praising someone they know. Over 21 days they sent this "surprise note" to 21 different people. The results? "Dramatically increased social connection," says Achor, adding that social connection is the biggest predictor of happiness in organizations. Oh, and teamwork improved as well.

"We've measured the collective IQ of teams and the collective years of experience of teams, but both of those metrics are trumped by social cohesion," says Achor.

Here's a fun challenge—write and send a quick thank-you each morning via e-mail or text, or USPS if you want to get fancy. Notice the daily or collective impact of engaging in this practice. Generating and sharing positive feelings can positively impact your mood in surprising ways—and make the day of the lucky recipient.

#56 Recruit Your Dream Team

WHY IT WORKS

Entrepreneur, author, and motivational speaker Jim Rohn has famously said that we are the average of the five people we spend the most time with. So, if we split our time between the office and home, we're essentially one-fifth our manager, one-fifth our assistant, one-fifth our spouse, one-fifth our mother-in-law, and one-fifth our two-year-old kid.

If we spend the majority of our time binge-watching the Kardashians, those five people just become Kim, Kourtney, Khloé, Kendall, and Kylie. Take that as you will.

Okay, so it's not 100 percent true that we "become" 20 percent of the people we're around most, but studies *do* show that we mirror the behaviors, gestures, body language, and affect of other people—even those we spend little time with. And beyond mere mirroring, our habits—both "good" and "bad"—are highly influenced by those folks we choose to spend time with.

Meaning pick your friends, not your nose. Or rather: Pick friends who don't pick their nose. I kid! But in all seriousness, if you've got a bad habit you want to kick, don't pick or seek out friends who engage in it. Instead, spend more time with people who practice those good habits you'd like to develop.

More specifically, if you're eager to up your willpower game, spend time with those who value and exhibit strong self-control. And to that end, good news for those who struggle with this: An article from the Association for Psychological Science reports that individuals who lack self-control may actually "have a unique skill: the ability to pick up on self-control cues in others and use those cues to form adaptive relationships," according to three 2013 studies. The lead researcher of those studies, Catherine Shea, suggests that you *do* "get by with a little help from your friends."

Increasing your motivation and strengthening your self-control can be fun when you decide to hang with people who also prioritize their own growth. So, connect with people you admire. Talk to people who have the lifestyle you want. Pick people who are striving to better themselves, those around them, the world. Shine your brightest by connecting with those who are already lighting the way.

HOW TO DO IT

1. **Listen in.** The likelihood is you've got at least one or two people in your life right now who possess qualities you admire—determination, willpower, integrity, you name it. The more time we spend with those people, the more they impact us. Listen to the way they speak about their experiences, how they perceive looming challenges, or how they confront responsibilities. Remain open and curious. You don't have to robotically follow everything they say word for word—nor should you. Simply consider *what it is* you respect about the way they operate.

2. **Reflect and learn.** Consider how those people feel about their goals. Why might they feel that way? What can you learn from the way they think about their own aspirations? How might you shift certain thoughts or behaviors to align more with what *you* really want in regard to your own goals and habits?

3. **Journal your answer and let it direct you.** Once you've journaled your thoughts, carve out time with those in your network who meet the criteria you deem helpful. To broaden the possibilities, expand your circle (see strategy #57).

#57 Dream Up Your Dream Team

WHY IT WORKS

In strategy #56, we chatted about the benefits of creating a network of people who inspire you whom you can spend time with—ideally in person, or even online via video conferencing, for instance. That's right: If you're not physically close location-wise, you can always link up on the Internet with your faraway friends, perhaps even forming an online accountability group whose members support one another in sticking to their willpower habit.

Now let's take things one step further.

If you can't physically be with these people, you can still benefit from their athleticism, wisdom, style, grace—whatever qualities they have that you seek. When you're about to lose your cool or face an unforeseen obstacle and don't have anyone to turn to, merely envision these people—what they'd say when they want to control their anger, how they'd act when facing a challenge, what advice they'd give when confronted with uncertainty.

Am I totally imagining things? Yes. Am I inviting you to do the same? Double yes. Because by mentally recruiting the people who inspire you onto your willpower dream team, when the going gets tough, you'll have a pack of allies, comrades, and best friends there in the literal blink of an eye, supporting you through your most trying self-control efforts.

As I mentioned earlier, our minds can't *exactly* tell the difference between fact and fiction. That's why when we watch a rom-com we swoon, a horror movie we scream, a comedy we laugh. Although rationally, we understand what we're seeing isn't "real," our brain still partially believes these things are happening to us.

So, if our mind is assuming fiction is fact, why not make fact fantastical? Dream up incredible, inspiring people who can cheer you on and support your best efforts, even if only in your mind. If your brain can't quite tell the difference, you might as well recruit and employ the best willpower support team one could dream of.

HOW TO DO IT

1. **Redirect your vision.** Unsolicited and gratuitous advice is everywhere you turn. Whether in the news, on TV, or on social media, there's a lot of funny business that's easy to make our business. Take an honest look at who or what isn't currently serving you. Where our mind goes, our energy flows—meaning if you want to become inspired, flow on over to things that inspire you.

2. **Choose your teammates.** Think of five people who make you want to do better and be better. Write their names on a sheet of paper. Invite them to the proverbial table. Consider them your trusted advisors. The Mr. Miyagi to your Karate Kid. The Rafiki to your Simba. The Yoda to your Luke. The goal is not for them to replace your own inner knowledge of what's right for you. Instead, consider them mentors you can figuratively turn to for advice or to cheer, bolster, and guide you toward decisions that will serve you best.

3. **Call them in.** When you've got a problem, a quandary, a challenge that needs solving, mentally tune in and envision your dream team of trusted advisors. Let them help, encourage, support, and guide you through.

#58 *Understand Impulses*

WHY IT WORKS

I once had a client we'll call Deborah, who would sit at her desk, open her laptop, and create marketing materials for her coaching practice. If she ever got stuck while writing, though, she'd suddenly find herself online shopping instead. A pause would lead to perusing the website of her favorite store. When she stagnated, she spent! Her wardrobe was growing, but the needle wasn't moving as fast as we'd have liked on her business. "It's not like I want to," she told me. "It just always kind of . . . happens."

We all know Deborah. We've all *been* Deborah. Ready to focus but _____ ←(insert your vice of choice here) instead.

Whether or not we too are trigger-happy shoppers, at some point we've experienced an impulse, urge, need, or desire that typically swiftly overcomes us. All of a sudden we're a puppet, ordering that third mimosa, scarfing down the last of the potato chips, doing the bidding of an often nonsensical puppet master.

Psychologist and MacArthur Fellow Angela Duckworth discusses three ways this sly "puppeteer" gains control, or as she might put it, how impulses turn into actions. In her study "Beyond Willpower: Strategies for Reducing Failures of Self-Control," Duckworth shares that substance use, for example, "can be triggered by the sight of friends smoking marijuana at a party, rewarded by acceptance from peers and drug-induced feelings of pleasure, and negatively reinforced with reduction in peer pressure."

When you break it down, these reactions make total sense. We're triggered when we see it, we're accepted when we smoke it, and we're relieved when we're not punished for not engaging in it—which makes doing it beyond understandable! We're rewarded with the ultimate trifecta—desire, acceptance, relief—all by saying four simple words: "Sure, I'll have some."

By understanding and learning about what triggers us, about when and how we become impulsive, and about what reinforces or undermines our decisions, we can become more thoughtful. This can help us uphold our long-term goal instead of prioritizing the short-term relief that comes with, for example, buying eight sweaters at a time.

HOW TO DO IT

1. **Identify the things that make you go *hmm*.** Become familiar with the things that send a jolt of dopamine to your system—checking your social media or dating apps or ordering that second or third drink. When you know what triggers you, you can . . .

2. **Plan for it, ahead of time.** Think, "When I go to the party and am offered a drink, I'm going to already have a soda in hand and say no." Implement if-then statements (see strategy #6, page 32).

3. **Scale your impulses.** Distinguish between those nice-to-haves ("It might be nice to shop, but I can stay focused, too"), need-to-haves ("It is necessary I indulge"), and want-to-haves ("I really want this, but I might be able to ride the urge and do without"). When you can determine which is which, you'll be able to pinpoint how to proceed in the moment.

#59 *Meditate to Activate*

WHY IT WORKS

Ever raced home to cook a healthy meal for the family while on a work call, pushing a stroller, and walking your shih tzu? Maybe the circumstance and dog breed were different, but at some point or another, we've all felt overwhelmed and multitasked to get it all done. Yet when you find yourself feeling hectic and hurried, slowing down and focusing on your breath may actually help you speed things up.

Scientists have found that training in mindfulness-oriented meditation can strengthen our ability to repeatedly focus our attention. Brain-scan studies demonstrate that when we meditate, we turn down those scattered or wandering thoughts and switch on our brain's prefrontal cortex—home to none other than our friend willpower.

Meaning? *Meditation creates greater focus.* So when you're eager to complete a time-sensitive or challenging task but can't seem to concentrate? Stop what you're doing, drop into a seated, cross-legged position, and close your eyes. And remember to focus on your breath.

HOW TO DO IT

1. **Sit comfortably with your spine straight and eyes closed.** If crossing your legs isn't comfortable for you, find a position that is.

2. **Take slow breaths.** Breathe slowly: in through your nose, then out through your mouth.

3. **If thoughts enter your mind, lovingly watch them go by.** Perhaps picture each thought like a leaf floating down a river (or chose your own imagery)—then return to your slow, deep breathing.

#60 Change Your Thoughts, Change Your Results

WHY IT WORKS

As part of your willpower habit, you've decided to defriend an uber-sweet frenemy. Your freezer, once home to ice-cream containers of her, is now a frozen-veggie haven. Your cookie jar—now filled with fruit. That hidden bedroom stash—tossed!

That's right. It's a chocolate breakup. And it's *so* official when, alas! The "likeliest" of events occurs when you're chosen to chaperone a school trip to Hersheypark, Pennsylvania.

"Darn!" you think. "Might as well stay committed to my chocolate GF until after the trip." Right?

Circumstances—perhaps not as unlikely as this—will arise, making it *seem* impossible to stick to our willpower habit. The truth is, though, while we can't always control the circumstance, we can control our thoughts about it.

One person may view this day in Hersheypark as an insurmountable obstacle, where avoiding eating gobs of chocolate is useless. Another may view this chocolate field trip as an opportunity to practice their willpower, preparing by fueling up with a protein-packed meal before touring the sites.

In each example the circumstance—going to Hersheypark—is the same. Yet having different thoughts about the circumstance could create much different results. There's no one right way. But, staying with an ex after the relationship's over never feels that great.

HOW TO DO IT

1. **Become aware of the thoughts that are triggered by certain circumstances.** For example, you might think, "I'm going to be *so* tempted," when considering all the sweets in Hersheypark.

2. **Decide whether you'd like to change those thoughts and what different thoughts would better support you.** You might decide to focus on the beauty of the area and fun with your friend.

3. **Think about the feeling you'd experience from choosing that new, supportive thought.** Perhaps you'd feel mindful and excited!

4. **What positive action might you take based on that feeling?** You could take pictures and go on exhilarating rides.

Engineer Your Desired Results

Hoping for a certain outcome? Here's a nifty acronym and way to reverse engineer the result you want most. Simply plug your desired result into the following equation, then work backward to determine the necessary thoughts, feelings, and actions to get you there.

RAFT = RESULTS ← ACTIONS create ← FEELINGS create ← THOUGHTS create

R: Result. What *result* do you desire most? (A clean bedroom.)

A: Action. What *action* might support achieving that result? (Vacuuming and picking up clothes.)

F: Feeling. What *feeling* might you generate to inspire taking that action? (Determined.)

T: Thought. What *thought* might help create that feeling? (I can totally do this in 10 minutes.)

Try out the RAFT formula to get you to your desired results!

#61 Resolve Cognitive Dissonance

WHY IT WORKS

You enjoy smoking but know it's bad for you. You buy a suit for an event even though you consider it way too pricey. You, my friend, are experiencing something called "cognitive dissonance"—basically holding two contradictory beliefs at the same time. It's kind of like you're a cheerleader for two opposing teams, which can be confusing on game day.

Our mind seeks harmony, so if we spend time in disaccord, maintaining oppositional beliefs, values, or ideas, our mind will want to move toward alignment.

So, what does this mean for our willpower habit? Well, if we're in a negotiation, the most confident, strong, or compelling argument is likely to win. Similarly, when you're experiencing the mental discomfort of cognitive dissonance—for instance, "should I or shouldn't I overspend?"—and want to escape it, just pick a winner, build a stronger case for said winner, and strike the gavel.

Yet, it's not quite as easy as 1, 2, 3, especially if you've become comfortable with the discomfort that comes with saying yes to two opposing sides. It's like being the child of two continually bickering parents. You may be used to the situation, but likely you haven't felt much peace lately. Luckily, you can use the mental discomfort of cognitive dissonance to help motivate you toward your goal.

HOW TO DO IT

1. **Acknowledge yourself.** So, you've been rooting for two teams. It's totally okay! Both have served a certain purpose for you. That suit was gorgeous. Inhaling the cigarettes really did feel great. Yet, you recognize saving the money and your lungs are nice options, too.

2. **Pick a team.** Decide which team you want to be on most. Take off the other team's colors and go root for the one you think the *real* winner is or should be.

3. **Have empathy for yourself during this process.** When you've spent time cheering for two teams, letting one go most likely won't be easy. You may question your choice or try going back to reconcile with keeping both. Remember: If you've been 50/50, even a move to 60/40 could make you feel squeamish! Yet, you know what you really want, deep down. Stay the course. Keep cheering on the team you really want to win. Go, Team Healthy Lungs! And sooner rather than later, you'll be able to tip your hat to the other team while knowing the team you chose is the one that reflects the best of you.

#62 *Cultivate Desire*

WHY IT WORKS

We're here reading this because we want to do things differently. We want to stop smoking. We want to quit spending. We want to start speaking up. But . . . *why*? What would it actually do for us if we accomplished those things? Close your eyes and really picture it—no longer having to excuse ourselves from that engaging conversation to go have a cigarette. No longer logging into our bank account and thinking, "Of course I spent more than I wanted." Instead, feeling abundant, *always*. Embracing the present moment, *consistently*. Saying what we've wanted to say to the person we've wanted to say it to, *finally*.

In the moment we're debating speaking up or remaining silent or staying in the conversation or leaving to smoke, it's easy to prioritize instant gratification—to satisfy that pressing need for nicotine now. Instead, let's forgo what we crave in the short term for a beautiful long-term solution for what we *really* want, what we more deeply crave: a sustainable, lasting way of being.

In her book *The Willpower Instinct*, Kelly McGonigal writes that when giving in is more tempting than ever, you should access your "want power," the motivation that "gives you strength when you feel weak." If you're feeling particularly tempted, remind yourself why your goal matters—not just why you think it should matter, according to McGonigal. For instance, instead of thinking, "I *should* get healthy" or "I *should* want to write," think about why health or writing truly does matter to you (see strategy #43, page 96).

When willpower is depleted, tapping into that want power can light up parts of your prefrontal cortex, lending you fuel simply from being inspired.

HOW TO DO IT

1. **Alleviate the pressure**. When we feel under the gun to make a decision—to eat the cookie or not, for instance—we'll likely make a stress-based choice. Instead, breathe, relax, and then . . .

2. **Zoom out!** Yep, like a camera lens going from focusing in on one tree to pulling out and seeing the entire forested landscape. Contextualize this moment in time as just that: *one* moment in time. It doesn't define you. Instead of zooming in on this one choice, zoom out and remember this is just one step on your way to the thing that really matters to you, like being healthy enough to play with your grandkids. Replace the reality of what's currently in front of you with *that ideal image*—you and them on a swing set: playing, enjoying, laughing. Remember this isn't really about some starch and carbs rolled into some circular shape we call a cookie. It's future moments, experiences. It's love.

3. **Find solace.** After remembering your why, Kelly McGonigal suggests considering others—for example, your kids and grandkids and how progressing toward what you really want will benefit them as well. How will not smoking, not overindulging, help those you love, too? Get creative in your thinking and find solace in solutions that ultimately benefit everyone.

#63 Get Your Beauty Rest

WHY IT WORKS

A night of tossing and turning or getting only a couple hours of sleep is so not fun. *Especially* when you have to work the next day. *Double especially* when that work requires your complete focus and best foot forward.

Admittedly, many of us can't drop into a deep slumber on demand. But we can do our part to set ourselves up for sleep success. And the point isn't only to catch some z's. As it turns out, a good sleep regimen—sticking to a consistent sleep/wake schedule and getting sufficient, good-quality sleep—may be more critical to our functioning than food! If we went several days without food, we'd likely be weak, hungry, and agitated. However, several days without sleep would render us almost entirely unable to function. Even tiny amounts of sleep deprivation can mean diminished physical and psychological resources.

So, if we're prioritizing increasing our willpower, let alone our ability to speak in complete sentences and not use our office desk calendar as a pillow, don't forgo getting your beauty rest! For improved sleep hygiene, consider the following tips from the National Sleep Foundation.

HOW TO DO IT

1. **Take a nap.** A quick catnap (less than 30 minutes) can improve your performance.

2. **Get into a bedtime routine that enhances relaxation.** This might mean taking some time to read, meditate, or whatever helps you unwind.

3. **Avoid bright lights or electronics before bed.** If you wake up in the middle of the night, resist checking your phone, as this type of light activates the brain.

4. **Avoid stimulants close to bedtime.** This includes caffeine and nicotine, as well as late heavy meals that can cause discomfort from indigestion.

5. **Make sure your mattress and pillows are right for you.** Keep the room dark and the temperature cool (between 60°F and 67°F).

#64 Read a Quote

WHY IT WORKS

"What is now proved was once only imagined."—William Blake
"Willpower is a muscle. The more you use it, the stronger it gets."—Unknown
"The willingness to show up changes us. It makes us a little braver each time."—Brené Brown

If you just read these three quotes, your willpower is *officially* stronger! Okay, maybe not officially, but here's some good news if you love quotes (or use social media). You know those eye-catching photos on Instagram—the pineapple with the "Life's sweet" text, or better yet, the runner with the inspiring quote that reads, "It isn't where you came from. It's where you're going that counts"? Just *reading* quotes on willpower can strengthen your willpower.

In a 2017 study, willpower depletion was counteracted when participants simply read famous quotes on willpower. Now, the test group of this study was mostly women and college-aged students, but men and seniors (or 30-, 40-, and 50-somethings), don't fret! An earlier study done on positive emotion found that participants exposed to subliminal positive stimuli were similarly able to self-regulate for longer after ego depletion.

So, how does reading quotes on willpower actually increase willpower? One reason has to do with values. If you focus on a quote that reinforces your values, you help inspire and anchor yourself in what's most important to you (see strategy #43, page 96).

HOW TO DO IT

1. **Select several quotes on willpower that resonate with or motivate you.** You might jot down quotes you find inspiring when you read, save inspirational Instagram posts, or pick up a book of quotes.

2. **Frame those quotes, hang them in your office, or even make them a desktop screensaver or phone background.** That way, you'll be able to see them throughout the day.

3. **Repeat a quote.** Try repeating a particularly meaningful quote to yourself when you meditate or whenever you're feeling unmotivated and in need of some inspiration.

#65 Fuel Up with the Right Foods

WHY IT WORKS

In a study with three groups of high-school students, one group was instructed to eat low-glycemic foods such as oatmeal, fruit, and eggs, while another group ate high-glycemic foods like bagels and Pop-Tarts. The third group ate no food at all. When measured by teachers on behavior and academic performance, the low-glycemic group significantly outperformed the others.

Meaning eat well to do well!

Incorporating foods that are particularly rich sources of healthy components, such as omega-3 fatty acids, B vitamins, beta-carotene, and antioxidants, is a great place to start. Numerous studies have demonstrated that these elements support your heart and blood vessels, as well as your brain health.

HOW TO DO IT

Plan a healthy diet. There are plenty of resources to help you plan a healthy diet. The following types of foods are the ones that most experts agree are key: leafy green vegetables (kale, spinach, collards, broccoli), fatty fish (salmon, canned tuna packed in water, cod), berries (blueberries, blackberries, strawberries), nuts (almonds, walnuts), seeds (chia, pumpkin, flax), vitamin C–rich foods (oranges, bell peppers, guava, tomatoes), healthy fats (olive oil, avocados), and coffee and tea. Some experts promote additional foods, such as lean meat, eggs, turmeric, and dark chocolate. Consider getting the all-clear from your health care professional before making big changes to your diet.

Everyday Temptations: An Experience Study

In a 2012 study from the University of Chicago Booth School of Business, researchers monitored 208 men and women in a German city. At random intervals, a beeper would go off, and the participants had to report on any desires they felt at the moment and within the prior half hour. If they experienced desire, they had to report its object, strength, and duration. Most importantly, they had to resist the urge to pursue that desire.

More than 10,000 reports were collected. From those, 7,827 desire reports were generated. The most frequent desires were to eat and drink, sleep, and enjoy leisure, sex, and other kinds of interactions, such as checking e-mail and social networking sites. Remarkably, the researchers concluded that people spend at least four hours a day experiencing and resisting desires.

Their most popular method to resist temptation was to seek a distraction or start a new activity, although they also tried direct suppression.

#66 *Find Your Focus*

WHY IT WORKS

Write the newsletter. Grade the papers. Call the babysitter. Shoot the video. Without a personal assistant, an on-call copywriter, and five pairs of hands, is multitasking the next best option when our plate is full?

Bouncing from one task to another, back and forth like a ping-pong game, can leave us with what University of Washington business professor Sophie Leroy calls "attention residue" in her 2016 study. This is when your brain is still partially focused on that initial task, although you've shifted your attention to that next item up to bat.

If we want to perform optimally, Leroy suggests we need to focus entirely on that new task. Think of it like a laptop with multiple tabs left open. Exiting out of one window before opening the next will help our computer run faster and be more effective.

HOW TO DO IT

1. **Plan to focus on the task at hand by avoiding distractions.** Can we plan for every distraction? Not always—see strategy #6, page 32—but we'll likely be surprised at how much freedom, time, and room we have once we clear the decks and simply focus on what's right in front of us.

2. **Block off a set, specific amount of time for each task.** Temptation-proof your environment—see strategy #37, page 86—meaning hire the babysitter, close the door, turn off your phone. Minimize potential interruptions.

3. **Finish one task before starting another.** When you completely finish the task at hand before starting the next, you're more likely to knock both out of the park.

#67 Shift Your Focus

WHY IT WORKS

In strategy #66, we learned the downside of distraction and bouncing from task to task. But, fear not, my frenzied friend! If you *do* become distracted, you might also become *creative*.

According to a 2017 article from researchers at Columbia Business School, task-switching—particularly between two creative tasks, like designing a business logo or knitting a scarf—actually alleviates cognitive fixation and boosts creativity. When you step away from the original task and plug into something new and different, you prime your mind to begin generating fresh, innovative ideas instead of remaining stuck and stagnant.

Now, you may be asking yourself which is better: what we learned in strategy #66 (stick with a task to completion to perform optimally) or what this strategy encourages (switch to a different task and potentially increase creativity).

The choice is yours! Perhaps it's like this: "When I crave creativity, I switch tasks. When I want to perform optimally, I stay on (the initial) task." You can't go wrong, so try both out. Either way, you'll learn, course correct, and become more creative. And productive.

HOW TO DO IT

Recognize when to switch things up. Particularly when working on tasks involving creativity, feeling stagnant or fresh out of ideas after a while is natural. When you recognize or even plan for a possible decline in idea generation, you no longer have to stay stuck. Even if you're not finished with the activity, if you're hitting a wall, switch to something different, then circle back to the original task—and view it with fresh eyes.

#68 Go All In

WHY IT WORKS

You're reading this on purpose. It's not because you're kinda sorta interested and you kinda sorta want to achieve your goal. It's because there's a part of you that recognizes you're not just "kinda sorta" but actually completely and incredibly capable. *Unquestionably*.

Now, if you're standing by a cold pool and want to learn to swim, dipping your toe in first might seem like the most intelligent choice. Not fully committing to a willpower habit but trying it out. Testing the waters. But wading, wavering, and putting on floaties may be more psychologically demanding than taking a new route—and that's simply diving in.

Committing to yourself. Fully. Committing to what you want. Completely.

"The best moments in our lives are not the passive, receptive, relaxing times," says Mihaly Csikszentmihalyi, who identified the concept of flow state (see strategy #34, page 79). "The best moments usually occur if a person's body or mind is stretched to its limits in a voluntary effort to accomplish something difficult and worthwhile."

The *best* moments. You deserve a best moment. A leap. A dive. Feeling the cold but laughing at how different and beautiful it is, all at the same time.

HOW TO DO IT

1. **Commit to yourself and your goal.** A study by the American Society for Training and Development found that consciously deciding to complete a goal increases your probability of completing it by 25 percent.

2. **Tell someone about it.** If you commit to someone by telling them that you will do it, that percentage increases to 65 percent.

3. **Set an accountability appointment with that someone.** If you have a specific accountability appointment with that someone, your probability of completing the goal becomes a whopping 95 percent!

#69 *Picture the Possibilities*

WHY IT WORKS

Let's say you have a choice: comfort or discomfort. Which would you pick? Probably comfort, right? It *feels* better. Now let's say you learned discomfort—while it wouldn't feel so great—would ultimately get you to your goal. Comfort would just get you more of the same.

The plot thickens . . .

It's easy to rationalize why our cycle of overspending, undercharging, or putting off learning that new language isn't *that bad*. We've put up with it this far, so what's a few more weeks, months, or years?

Well, imagine it is 10 years from now, and exactly 10 years ago you decided to choose possibility. You slowly but surely began saving. You raised your rates in your service-based business. You signed up for that French class. Now, 10 years later, you're living the reality of those earlier choices.

You're teaching your kids to speak French. The financial stress you once regularly experienced no longer impacts you. Or perhaps your friendships are no longer draining or overly demanding because you decided to nurture new ones and actively spend time with different people.

Our future isn't set in stone. It can be a blank canvas we can paint any color. To do so requires a belief in future possibility. It requires embracing the initial discomfort of choosing a color we've never used before but have always been intrigued by.

HOW TO DO IT

1. **Envision the future.** Instead of putting up with what's kind of working in your life, picture fresh, new possibilities for your future. Focus on the results that would be most

incredible—going from feeling like a stressed, tired parent, for example, to becoming an active, happy one. Or moving from experiencing nagging "I should be healthier" thoughts to enjoying eating well, and, for instance, biking regularly with friends.

2. **Think long term.** Emphasize the long-term gain of reaching your goals instead of the short-term discomfort that may come with committing to something new. Do this by visualizing all the exciting realities that could materialize when you choose to move toward what you truly desire for your life. Choose that new possibility, pick up a fresh paintbrush, and make your mark.

#70 Marry the "Trying" with the "Tried-and-True"

WHY IT WORKS

Doing the dishes, taking out the trash. Just because they're tasks we *have to do* doesn't mean we *have to dread* doing 'em! The key is a concept called "activity pairing," our ticket for turning those have-tos into want-tos by marrying the "trying" with the "tried-and-true." Also called "temptation bundling," coupling something you enjoy with something that challenges you may alleviate anxiousness or avoidance around engaging in that more difficult task.

In a 2012 study, participants were given enticing audiobooks that some were encouraged to—and others limited to—use exclusively at the gym. Initial gym visitation increased 51 percent and 29 percent, respectively, and when the study concluded, 61 percent of participants decided to purchase gym-only access to the audiobooks. This suggests the desirability/effectiveness of bundling "want" experiences with "should" experiences.

HOW TO DO IT

1. **Identify those more challenging "shoulds" that you are building into your willpower habit.** These are the ones you may typically avoid. Ironing your clothes? Not ordering fries with that?

2. **Create a list of enjoyable or "want-to" activities.** Watching soap operas? Playing basketball?

3. **Dramatically increase the probability of completing "shoulds" by pairing them with "wants."** In other words, put those

activities together. Listen to your favorite podcast *only* when you're doing laundry, for example. Or get a pedicure while writing thank-you notes.

What the Judge Ate for Breakfast

A 2011 study called "Extraneous Factors in Judicial Decisions" brought the phrase "what the judge ate for breakfast" into question. Ironically, researchers of the study actually did question whether what the judge ate influenced their verdicts!

Results showed that favorable rulings on parole decisions among experienced judges dropped, little by little, from around 65 percent to zero as time passed after breakfast and/or lunch breaks.

Meaning? First, resting and replenishing mental resources through glucose may strengthen your mood and willpower when you're feeling drained, and second, if you're ever in trouble with the law, try seeing the judge right after lunch.

#71 *Embrace the Freedom to Fail*

WHY IT WORKS

Pitfalls and setbacks are understandable when you're trying something new. But instead of thinking of these stumbling blocks as bad, wrong, or just plain unacceptable, or making them a reason to quit, celebrate them! Strange concept, right?

According to Martin Seligman, the "father" of positive psychology (the scientific study of "what makes life worth living"), "it's not our failures that determine our future success, but how we explain it to ourselves."

Imagine that! If the way we get to success is by putting a positive spin on failures, why not view failure as an indication that we're trying instead of making it evidence that we're not doing well? Why not celebrate when we put one foot in front of the other, regardless of the outcome? Because regardless of the outcome, we're moving forward.

HOW TO DO IT

Remember your growth mindset (see page 10). Instead of tracking success by the things you might typically consider successful—avoiding the donut, not overspending—redefine success as the effort you put into your actions (i.e., "I took the stairs instead of the elevator, even though I was tired"). Remember, action over traction! Forward momentum itself can be greater than results.

#72 *Affirm Yourself*

WHY IT WORKS

If you've ever told yourself—even subconsciously—"I can't" or "I'll fail" or "I'll just push this off" when it comes to creating change, you're so not alone! We all have this inner critic who tends to feed us doubt or worry in a misguided effort to protect us (see strategy #22, page 58). What this means, though, is while we may finally be ready to say yes to developing our willpower, the prospect of actually doing so might feel uncomfortable. Committing to any new path requires thinking fresh, productive thoughts—sometimes in the complete opposite direction of what we're used to believing—such as "I can" and "I'll achieve" and "I'll keep going."

What this means is change goes beyond just *doing* something differently. It's simultaneously *choosing to believe* we can.

Fortunately, there are so many ways to strengthen your self-belief, including using affirmations or positive sayings like "I have the ability to succeed at what I put my mind to" or "I'm a confident, capable individual." Now, perhaps you already believe these things, or perhaps these ideas are new ones that you'd simply *like* to believe. Either way, by writing down your affirmations, reading them aloud, or repeating them to yourself, you can direct your mind toward possibility and growth.

Particularly when facing adversity, affirmations can help promote open-mindedness, support us in maintaining self-control, and even help quell apprehension so that we can successfully meet and overcome obstacles.

So, if we're confronted with an obstacle, a new choice, or an alternative route along our willpower journey, we can address rather than avoid that hurdle. We can remember that we are capable of rising to new challenges.

HOW TO DO IT

1. **Consult your present self.** Create a list of affirmations that you currently believe about yourself: "I am trying something new" or "I am open to enjoying this process" or "I've succeeded in the past and can succeed now."

2. **Consult your future self.** What sort of affirmations might your future self believe? They could be "I love being cigarette-free" or "I enjoy feeling healthy and going to the gym."

3. **Select your affirmations.** If you need some in-the-moment encouragement, use the affirmations you already believe. Say them out loud to yourself or record them in a voice note and listen back to them on repeat. If you are seeking inspiration and drive, use the future-self affirmations. Envision you're already your future self and affirm what will be true in the future!

#73 Embrace Mindfulness

WHY IT WORKS

Mindfulness is like this hidden gem of a tool anyone can use, particularly when experiencing negative emotions like anxiety or regret. Tap into mindfulness and suddenly you're present, in the here and now, feeling things as subtle as the air on your skin or tuning into the faint smell of a fragrant flower. Future anxieties or past worries slip away, replaced by calm, peace, and a sense of ease.

Dreamy moments like these are yours for the taking whenever you might want or really need them. Imagine you're invited to a party but have work to complete. Perhaps you feel anxiety, worrying, "If I say no, will I ever get invited again?" Or maybe you default to procrastination, thinking, "I usually don't say yes. I can put off this project anyway."

Instead, remember your buddy mindfulness. By practicing it, you're able to ground yourself, embrace the present moment, take in the environment through all of your senses, and enter a state of relaxation and maybe even joy.

Now, mindfulness won't make the decision for you. But after experiencing it, it's likely you'll respond to the question from a more knowing, perceptive, intuitive place.

HOW TO DO IT

1. **Think of mindfulness as less of a "to-do" and more of a "to-be."** You don't have to sign up for a yoga class or mindfulness retreat to embrace it. Mindfulness merely means enhancing your awareness or consciousness around something—being in the present moment and taking note of your thoughts, feelings, and any bodily sensations as they arise.

2. **Practice with everyday experiences.** If you're eating, slow down and concentrate on the flavors, aromas, and textures of your food. Describe them in your mind. If you're in a park, notice the sun on your skin, the sounds of kids playing around you. If you're on a busy street, see the traffic controller flail their arms, the cars honk their horns. You don't have to control the environment or react to it. Just notice it.

#74 *Understand Patterns and Triggers*

WHY IT WORKS

It's quite easy to spend our days on autopilot, doing what we need to do to get the job done. However, when we make a conscious effort not just to *do* but to watch ourselves *doing*, we increase the likelihood of making choices that support our willpower efforts and may even help increase happiness in our day-to-day lives! (See strategy #36, page 84.)

We can do this by using a little process called "self-monitoring," intentionally and consistently observing our behavior.

When we take a step back and put on our observer hat, we give ourselves the space to understand ourselves—our feelings, our behaviors—in a whole new way. Think, "Oh! My husband just made a small dig at me, no wonder I went for a second dinner roll!" When you wear your observer hat and begin having more of these insights, you're going to remember that when you're triggered, you do *not*, for example, have to eat that donut. Instead, you can replace the "small dig = eat a carb" equation with "small dig = speak up to your husband"—particularly if speaking up is part of your will-power habit.

No matter the trigger, self-monitoring proves to be a powerful tool for positive change. It's even been shown to help students improve academically and help those who struggle with alcohol drink less.

HOW TO DO IT

Instead of acting on emotion, consider why you're feeling it.
Observe your thoughts, feelings, and behaviors and begin to understand how they might trigger positive or negative actions (see the sidebar "Engineer Your Desired Results," page 127).

#75 Get Your Yoga Fix

WHY IT WORKS

After attending a yoga class *just once a week* over the course of six weeks, participants in a randomized control trial at a British university self-reported mood and well-being increases. These newbie yogis described that the benefits went beyond just "clear-mindedness, composure, elation, energy, and confidence"—yes, they reported *all* of those things—to also include "increased life purpose and satisfaction, and feelings of greater self-confidence during stressful situations."

Dusts off yoga mat and signs up for next class.

Meaning we don't have to get promoted, get engaged, or bend over backward (depending on the type of yoga) to experience these superfluous positive feelings. According to this study, practicing Dru yoga—just one hour a week for a little over a month—could, simply put, make you happier.

So, stretching, balancing, and holding your left foot—how does it all have such a remarkable impact on us? And beyond the slew of positive emotions we experience, how does yoga result in greater focus? According to Roy Baumeister, practicing self-control leads to more self-control (see strategy #45, page 99)—even and especially practicing small acts of self-control such as "monitoring and improving postures."

Countless similar studies have shown yoga's use of physical activity, breath control, relaxation exercises, and meditation practices enhances physiological and psychological well-being. And it turns out that millions of people caught onto this fact long ago! Our "yogi ancestors" have practiced yoga as a form of health promotion over the span of many centuries.

We can learn a thing or two from these yogis of centuries past. When your stress is up, drop into Downward-Facing Dog. Perfect your asanas, find stillness in savasana, and watch yourself become clearer, reenergized, and even elated.

HOW TO DO IT

1. **Find a studio.** Not all yoga studios are created equal. Experiment and find a studio or teacher you enjoy.

2. **Make a studio.** You don't necessarily have to leave your home to up your resilience. Purchase a yoga mat, find a yoga YouTuber, or even hire a private teacher if you're so inclined, and practice in the comfort of your own home.

3. **Practice your posture.** If you can't seem to find the time to incorporate yoga into your schedule (see strategy #29, page 70), simply work on your posture at home. If you practice sitting up straighter, or even invest in and use a posture corrector, you'll simultaneously be increasing your self-control.

Laugh It Out!

When you're feeling down, it's hard to concentrate on your goals. It may sound funny, but laughter therapy has become a recognized therapy for promoting mental wellness! Studies have examined the efficacy of different types of laughter, including their triggers:

Genuine or spontaneous (by external stimuli)

Simulated (by oneself at will)

Stimulated (by physical contact, such as tickling)

Induced (by drugs or other substances)

Pathological (no specific stimulus)

It's no surprise that genuine laughter has physiological and psychological benefits. But even the simulated laughter taught in laughter therapy has been shown to promote wellness. Laughter therapy has positively impacted individuals in numerous settings, from elderly participants at a South Korean community center to HIV-affected families in South Africa.

You can learn more online or from individuals certified in laughter therapy. In the meantime, seek out laughter to boost your wellness game—and thus, your willpower!

Resources

Interested in learning more about willpower and related topics? For information about what researchers have found, take a look at some of the articles listed in this book's References section.

For more general reading, there are many worthwhile resources. Here are a few to get you started!

American Psychological Association Psychology Help Center. "What You Need to Know about Willpower: The Psychological Science of Self-Control." https://www.apa.org/helpcenter/willpower.

Barker, Eric. *Barking Up the Wrong Tree: The Surprising Science behind Why Everything You Know about Success is (Mostly) Wrong.* New York: HarperOne, 2017.

Barker, Eric. *Barking Up the Wrong Tree* (blog).: https://www.bakadesuyo.com.

Clear, James. *Atomic Habits: Tiny Changes, Remarkable Results: An Easy and Proven Way to Build Good Habits and Break Bad Ones.* New York: Avery, 2018.

Dweck, Carol S. *Mindset: The New Psychology of Success.* Updated ed. New York: Ballantine Books, 2016.

Gostick, Adrian, and Chester Elton. *What Motivates Me: Put Your Passions to Work.* Kamas, Utah: Culture Works Press, 2014.

References

Achor, Shawn. *The Happiness Advantage: How a Positive Brain Fuels Success in Work and Life*. New York: Currency, 2010.

Ackerman, Courtney E. "83 Benefits of Journaling for Depression, Anxiety, and Stress." Positive Psychology. Accessed September 2019. https://positivepsychology.com/benefits-of-journaling/#research-journaling.

Alcoba, Jesús, and Laura López. "On Finding the Source of Human Energy: The Influence of Famous Quotations on Willpower." *Europe's Journal of Psychology* 13, no. 4 (November 30, 2017): 708–16. doi:10.5964/ejop.v13i4.1372.

American Psychological Association Psychology Help Center. "What You Need to Know about Willpower: The Psychological Science of Self-Control." Accessed August 26, 2019. https://www.apa.org/helpcenter/willpower.

Association for Psychological Science. "Low on Self-Control? Surrounding Yourself with Strong-Willed Friends May Help." Accessed September 2019. https://www.psychologicalscience.org/news/releases/low-on-self-control-surrounding-yourself-with-strong-willed-friends-may-help.html.

Barker, Eric. "Dan Ariely's 6 New Secrets to Effectively Managing Your Time." *Business Insider*. Accessed September 2019. https://www.businessinsider.com/secrets-to-effectively-manage-your-time-2014-10.

Barker, Eric. "Harvard Research Reveals a Fun Way to Be More Successful." Observer. Accessed September 2019. https://observer.com/2015/04/harvard-research-reveals-a-fun-way-to-be-more-successful.

Baumeister, Roy F., Ellen Bratslavsky, Mark Muraven, and Dianne M. Tice. "Ego Depletion: Is the Active Self a Limited Resource?" *Journal of Personality and Social Psychology* 74, no. 5 (May 1998): 1252–65. doi:10.1037/0022-3514.74.5.1252.

Baumeister, Roy F., Kathleen D. Vohs, and Dianne M. Tice. "The Strength Model of Self-Control." *Current Directions in Psychological Science* 16, no. 6 (December 1, 2007): 351–55. doi:10.1111/j.1467-8721.2007.00534.x.

Bourn, Chris. "The Psychology of Referring to Yourself in the Third Person." MEL Magazine. Accessed September 2019. https://melmagazine.com/en-us/story/the-psychology-of-referring-to-yourself-in-the-third-person.

Breines, Juliana G., and Serena Chen. "Self-Compassion Increases Self-Improvement Motivation." *Personality and Social Psychology Bulletin* 38, no. 9 (May 29, 2012): 1133–43. doi:10.1177/0146167212445599.

Cho, Joohee. "Laughter Therapy Takes Off in South Korea." *ABC News*. Accessed September 2019. https://abcnews.go.com/Health/MindMoodNews/story?id=4406589&page=1.

Currey, Mason. *Daily Rituals: How Artists Work*. New York: Alfred A. Knopf, 2013.

Danzinger, Shai, Jonathan Levav, and Liora Avnaim-Pesso. "Extraneous Factors in Judicial Decisions." *PNAS: Proceedings of the National Academy of Sciences of the United States of America* 108, no. 17 (April 26, 2011): 6889–92. doi:10.1073/pnas.1018033108.

David, Susan. "How to Manage Your Inner Critic." *Harvard Business Review*. Accessed September 2019. https://www.hbr.org/2010/01/how-to-quiet-your-inner-critic.

de Manzano, Örjan, Töres Theorell, László Harmat, and Fredrik Ullén. "The Psychophysiology of Flow during Piano Playing." *Emotion* 10, no. 3 (June 2010): 301–11. doi:10.1037/a0018432.

Dickens, Leah, and David DeSteno. "The Grateful Are Patient: Heightened Daily Gratitude Is Associated with Attenuated Temporal Discounting." *Emotion* 16, no. 4 (June 2016): 421–25. doi: 10.1037/emo0000176.

Duhigg, Charles. *The Power of Habit: Why We Do What We Do in Life and Business*. New York: Random House, 2012.

Duckworth, Angela L., Katherine L. Milkman, and David Laibson. "Beyond Willpower: Strategies for Reducing Failures of Self-Control." *Psychological Science in the Public Interest* 19, no. 3 (February 13, 2019): 102–29. doi:10.1177/1529100618821893.

Dweck, Carol S. *Mindset: The New Psychology of Success*. New York: Ballantine Books, 2016.

Eagleson, Claire, Sarra Hayes, Andrew Mathews, Gemma Perman, and Colette R. Hirsch. "The Power of Positive Thinking: Pathological Worry Is Reduced by Thought Replacement in Generalized Anxiety Disorder." *Behaviour Research and Therapy* 78 (March 2016): 13–18. doi:10.1016/j.brat.2015.12.017.

Eisenhower. "Introducing the Eisenhower Matrix." Accessed October 31, 2019. https://www.eisenhower.me/eisenhower-matrix/.

Elliot, Andrew J., and Patricia G. Devine. "On the Motivational Nature of Cognitive Dissonance: Dissonance as Psychological Discomfort." *Journal of Personality and Social Psychology* 67, no. 3 (September 1994): 382–94. doi:10.1037/0022-3514.67.3.382.

EOC Institute. "The Ultimate Guide to Willpower and Meditation." Accessed October 2019. https://eocinstitute.org/meditation/boosting-willpower-self-discipline.

Feloni, Richard. "How Celebrity Life Coach Tony Robbins Started Working with President Bill Clinton." *Business Insider*. December 2, 2014. https://www.businessinsider.com/life-coach-tony-robbins-bill-clinton-2014-12.

Foster, Jennifer. "Whether You Think You Can . . . Or Whether You Think You Can't . . . You're Right!" Wall Street Insanity. Accessed August 26, 2019. https://wallstreetinsanity.com

/whether-you-think-you-can-or-whether-you-think-you-cant
-youre-right/.

Goleman, Daniel. *Emotional Intelligence: Why It Can Matter More
Than IQ*. New York: Bantam Books, 1995.

Gostick, Adrian, and Chester Elton. *The Carrot Principle: How the
Best Managers Use Recognition to Engage Their People, Retain
Talent, and Accelerate Performance*. New York: Free Press, 2007.

Grossman, Igor, Anna Dorfman, Harrison Oakes, Henri C. Santos,
Kathleen D. Vohs, and Abigail A. Scholer. "Training for Wisdom:
The Illeist Diary Method." *PsyArXiv* (May 7, 2019). doi:10.31234/osf
.io/a5fgu.

Groth, Aimee. "You're the Average of the Five People You Spend
the Most Time With." *Business Insider*. Accessed September 2019.
https://www.businessinsider.com/jim-rohn-youre-the-average
-of-the-five-people-you-spend-the-most-time-with-2012-7.

Harris, Peter R. "Self-Affirmation and the Self-Regulation of Health
Behavior Change." *Self and Identity* 10, no. 3 (June 3, 2011): 304–14.
doi:10.1080/15298868.2010.517963.

Hartfiel, Ned, Jon Havenhand, Sat Bir Khalsa, Graham Clarke, and
Anne Krayer. "The Effectiveness of Yoga for the Improvement
of Well-Being and Resilience to Stress in the Workplace."
Scandinavian Journal of Work, Environment and Health 37, no. 1
(January 2011): 70–76. doi:10.5271/sjweh.2916.

Harvard Health Publishing. "Foods Linked to Better Brainpower."
Accessed September 2019. https://www.health.harvard.edu
/mind-and-mood/foods-linked-to-better-brainpower.

Hatzipapas, Irene, Maretha J. Visser, and Estie Janse van Rensburg.
"Laughter Therapy as an Intervention to Promote Psychological
Well-Being of Volunteer Community Care Workers Working with
HIV-Affected Families." *SAHARA-J: Journal of Social Aspects of
HIV/AIDS* 14, no. 1 (November 23, 2017): 202-12. doi:10.1080/172903
76.2017.1402696.

Herschfield, Hal E., Daniel G. Goldstein, William F. Sharpe, Jesse Fox, Leo Yeykelis, Laura L. Carstensen, and Jeremy N. Bailenson. "Increasing Saving Behavior through Age-Progressed Renderings of the Future Self." *Journal of Marketing Research* 48 (March 6, 2019): S23–S37. doi:10.1509/jmkr.48.SPL.S23.

Hofmann, Wilhelm, Roy F. Baumeister, Georg Förster, and Kathleen D. Vohs. "Everyday Temptations: An Experience Sampling Study of Desire, Conflict, and Self-Control." *Journal of Personality and Social Psychology* 102, no. 6 (June 2012): 1318–35. doi:10.1037/a0026545.

International Coach Federation. "ICF Global Coaching Client Study: Executive Summary." April 2009. https://researchportal .coachfederation.org/Document/Pdf/190.pdf.

Job, Veronika, Gregory M. Walton, Katharina Bernecker, and Carol S. Dweck. "Beliefs about Willpower Determine the Impact of Glucose on Self-Control." *PNAS: Proceedings of the National Academy of Sciences of the United States of America* 110, no. 37 (September 10, 2013): 14837–42. doi:10.1073/pnas.1313475110.

Kanfer, Frederick H. "Self-Monitoring: Methodological Limitations and Clinical Applications." *Journal of Consulting and Clinical Psychology* 35, no. 2 (October 1970): 148–52. doi:10.1037/h0029874.

Kannan, Divya, and Heidi M. Levitt. "A Review of Client Self-Criticism in Psychotherapy." *Journal of Psychotherapy Integration* 23, no. 2 (June 2013): 166–78. doi:10.1037/a0032355.

Kelly, Mary Louise. "Daniel Pink's 'When' Shows the Importance of Timing throughout Life." *All Things Considered*, NPR, January 17, 2018. https://www.npr.org/2018/01/17/578666036 /daniel-pinks -when-shows-the-importance-of-timing-throughout-life.

Kenrick, Douglas T., Vladas Griskevicius, Steven L. Neuberg, and Mark Schaller. "Renovating the Pyramid of Needs: Contemporary Extensions Built upon Ancient Foundations." *Perspectives on Psychological Science* 5, no. 3 (May 18, 2010): 292–314. doi:10.1177/1745691610369469.

Kent, Shia T., Leslie A. McClure, William L. Crosson, Donna K. Arnett, Virginia G. Wadley, and Nalini Sathiakumar. "Effect of

Sunlight Exposure on Cognitive Function among Depressed and Non-Depressed Participants: A REGARDS Cross-Sectional Study." *Environmental Health* 8, no. 34 (July 28, 2009). doi:10.1186/1476-069X-8-34.

Kross, Ethan, Emma Bruehlman-Senecal, Jiyoung Park, Aleah Burson, Adrienne Dougherty, Holly Shablack, Ryan Bremner, Jason Moser, and Ozlem Ayduk. "Self-talk as a Regulatory Mechanism: How You Do It Matters." *Journal of Personality and Social Psychology* 1106, no. 2 (February 2014): 304–24. doi:10.1037/a0035173.

Lee, Kate E., Kathryn J. H. Williams, Leisa D. Sargent, Nicholas S. G. Williams, and Katherine A. Johnson. "40-Second Green Roof Views Sustain Attention: The Role of Micro-breaks in Attention Restoration." *Journal of Environmental Psychology* 42 (June 2015): 182–89. doi:10.1016/j.jenvp.2015.04.003.

Lerner, Jennifer S., Ye Li, Piercarlo Valdesolo, and Karim S. Kassam. "Emotion and Decision Making." *Annual Review of Psychology* 66 (January 2015): 799–823. doi:10.1146/annurev-psych-010213-115043.

Leroy, Sophie, and Aaron M. Schmidt. "The Effect of Regulatory Focus on Attention Residue and Performance during Interruptions." *Organizational Behavior and Human Decision Processes* 137 (November 2016): 218–35. doi:10.1016/j.obhdp.2016.07.006.

Lu, Jackson G., Modupe Akinola, and Malia F. Mason. "'Switching On' Creativity: Task Switching Can Increase Creativity by Reducing Cognitive Fixation." *Organizational Behavior and Human Decision Processes* 139 (March 2017): 63–75. doi:10.1016/j.obhdp.2017.01.005.

Ma, Xiao, Zi-Qi Yue, Zhu-Qing Gong, Hong Zhang, Nai-Yue Duan, Yu-Tong Shi, Gao-Xia Wei, and You-Fa Li. "The Effect of Diaphragmatic Breathing on Attention, Negative Affect and Stress in Healthy Adults." *Frontiers in Psychology* (June 6, 2017). doi:10.3389/fpsyg.2017.00874.

Maslow, A. H. "A Theory of Human Motivation." *Psychological Review* 50, no. 4 (July 1943): 370–96. doi:10.1037/h0054346.

McGonigal, Kelly. "How to Make Stress Your Friend." TED video. 2013. https://www.ted.com/talks/kelly_mcgonigal_how_to _make_stress_your_friend?utm_campaign=tedspread&utm _medium=referral&utm_source=tedcomshare.

McGonigal, Kelly. "The Problem with Progress: Why Succeeding at Your Goals Can Sabotage Your Willpower." *Psychology Today*. Accessed September 2019. https://www.psychologytoday.com /ca/blog/the-science-willpower/201112/the-problem-progress-why -succeeding-your-goals-can-sabotage-your.

McGonigal, Kelly. *The Willpower Instinct: How Self-Control Works, Why It Matters, and What You Can Do to Get More of It*. New York: Avery, 2013.

Merriam-Webster. "Willpower." Accessed August 26, 2019. https://www.merriam-webster.com/dictionary/willpower.

Middleton, Yale. "75 Motivational Michael Jordan Quotes." Addicted2Success. Accessed September 2019. https://addicted2success.com/quotes/75-motivational -michael-jordan-quotes.

Milkman, Katherine L., Julia A. Minson, and Kevin G. M. Volpp. "Holding the Hunger Games Hostage at the Gym: An Evaluation of Temptation Bundling." *Management Science* 60, no. 2 (November 6, 2013: 283–99. doi:10.1287/mnsc.2013.1784.

Mischel, Walter, and Ebbe B. Ebbesen. "Attention in Delay of Gratification." *Journal of Personality and Social Psychology* 16, no. 2 (October 1970): 329-37. doi:10.1037/h0029815.

Muraven, Mark, Heather Rosman, and Marylène Gagné. "Lack of Autonomy and Self-Control: Performance Contingent Rewards Lead to Greater Depletion." *Motivation and Emotion* 31, no. 4 (December 2007): 322–30. doi:10.1007/s11031-007-9073-x.

Nakamura, Jeanne, and Mihaly Csikszentmihalyi. "The Concept of Flow." In Mihaly Csikszentmihalyi, *Flow and the Foundations of Positive Psychology: The Collected Works of Mihaly Csikszentmihalyi,* 239–63. Dordrecht: Springer, 2014. doi:10.1007/978-94-017-9088-8_16.

National Sleep Foundation. "What Is Sleep Hygiene?" Accessed September 2019. https://www.sleepfoundation.org/articles /sleep-hygiene.

Newport, Cal. "The Science of Procrastination: Researchers Tackle Willpower and Our Ability to Control It." *Study Hacks Blog*. Accessed September 2019. https://www.calnewport.com/blog /2008/01/23/the-science-of-procrastination-researchers-tackle -willpower-and-our-ability-to-control-it.

Oaten, Megan, and Ken Cheng. "Longitudinal Gains in Self-Regulation from Regular Physical Exercise." *British Journal of Health Psychology* 11, no. 4 (December 24, 2010): 717–33. doi:10.1348/135910706X96481.

Parker-Pope, Tara. "Go Easy on Yourself, a New Wave of Research Urges." *New York Times*. Accessed September 2019. https://well .blogs.nytimes.com/2011/02/28/go-easy-on-yourself-a-new-wave -of-research-urges.

Patel, Sujan. "Why Feeling Uncomfortable Is the Key to Success." *Forbes*. Accessed September 2019. https://www.forbes.com/sites /sujanpatel/2016/03/09/why-feeling-uncomfortable-is-the-key-to -success/#6fef6d541913.

Paul, Annie Murphy. "Can You Instill Mental Toughness?" *Time*. Accessed September 2019. http://ideas.time.com/2012/04/19 /can-you-instill-mental-toughness.

Pilcher, June J., Drew M. Morris, Janet Donnelly, and Hayley B. Feigl. "Interactions between Sleep Habits and Self-Control." *Frontiers in Human Neuroscience* (May 11, 2015). doi:10.3389/fnhum.2015 .00284.

Pink, Daniel H. *When: The Scientific Secrets of Perfect Timing*. New York: Riverhead Books, 2019.

Querstret, Dawn, and Mark Cropley. "Assessing Treatments Used to Reduce Rumination and/or Worry: A Systematic Review." *Clinical Psychology Review* 33, no. 8 (December 2013): 996–1009. doi:10.1016/j.cpr.2013.08.004.

Resnick, Brian. "The Myth of Self-Control." Vox. Accessed September 2019. https://www.vox.com/science-and-health /2016/11/3/13486940/self-control-psychology-myth.

Rohn, Jim. "Rohn: Why You Should Keep a Journal." *Success*. Accessed September 2019. https://www.success.com/rohn -why-you-should-keep-a-journal.

Roomer, Jari. "How to Reach Flow State (Using 10 Flow State 'Triggers')." Medium. Accessed September 2009. https://medium .com/personal-growth-lab/how-to-reach-flow-state-using-10-flow -state-triggers-473aa28dc3e5.

Seligman, Martin E. P. "Building Resilience." *Harvard Business Review*. Accessed November 2019. https://hbr.org/2011/04 /building-resilience.

Shea, Catherine T., Erin K. Davisson, and Gráinne M. Fitzsimons. "Riding Other People's Coattails: Individuals with Low Self-Control Value Self-Control in Other People." *Psychological Science* 24, no. 6 (April 4, 2013): 1031-36. doi:10.1177/0956797612464890.

Sifferlin, Alexandra. "Here's an Easy Way to Become More Patient." *Time*. Accessed September 2019. https://time.com/4277661 /gratitude-patience-self-control.

Smith, Alexander McCall. *The Full Cupboard of Life*. New York: Pantheon Books, 2004.

Sofis, Michael J., Ale Carrillo, and David P. Jarmolowicz. "Maintained Physical Activity Induced Changes in Delay Discounting." *Behavior Modification* 41, no. 4 (December 29, 2016): 499–528. doi:10.1177/0145445516685047.

Stoewen, Debbie L. "Dimensions of Wellness: Change Your Habits, Change Your Life." *Canadian Veterinary Journal* 58, no. 8 (August 2017): 861–62.

Taylor, Shelley E., Lien B. Pham, Inna D. Rivkin, and David A. Armor. "Harnessing the Imagination: Mental Simulation, Self-Regulation, and Coping." *American Psychologist* 53, no. 4 (April 1998): 429–39. doi:10.1037//0003-066x.53.4.429.

Tice, Diane M., Roy F. Baumeister, Dikla Shmueli, and Mark Muraven. "Restoring the Self: Positive Affect Helps Improve Self-Regulation Following Ego Depletion." *Journal of Experimental Social Psychology* 43, no. 3 (May 2007): 379–84. doi:10.1016/j.jesp.2006.05.007.

Tierney, John. "Do You Suffer from Decision Fatigue?" *New York Times*. Accessed September 2019. https://www.nytimes.com/2011/08/21/magazine/do-you-suffer-from-decision-fatigue.html?pagewanted=all.

Tomasino, Barbara, and Franco Fabbro. "Increases in the Right Dorsolateral Prefrontal Cortex and Decreases in the Rostral Prefrontal Cortex Activation after 8 Weeks of Focused Attention Based Mindfulness Meditation" *Brain and Cognition* 102 (February 2016): 46–54. doi:10.1016/j.bandc.2015.12.004.

Tunikova, Oksana. "The Science of Willpower: How to Train Your Productivity Muscle." Medium. Accessed September 2019. https://medium.com/@tunikova_k/the-science-of-willpower-how-to-train-your-productivity-muscle-8b2738ce745b.

Vilhauer, Jennice. "How to Get What You Really Want." *Psychology Today*. Accessed September 2019. https://www.psychologytoday.com/us/blog/living-forward/201512/how-get-what-you-really-want.

Walters, Helen. "The Upside of Stress: Kelly McGonigal at TEDGlobal 2013." *TED*. Accessed September 2019. https://blog.ted.com/the-upside-of-stress-kelly-mcgonigal-at-tedglobal-2013.

Wang, Dan. "More Motivated in Minutes: 5 Science-Backed Tricks to Get You Going." *Buffer*. Accessed September 2019. https://open.buffer.com/increase-your-motivation-tips.

Ward, Taylor. "3 Reasons Successful Professionals Hire a Life Coach." Ladders. Accessed September 2019. https://www.theladders.com/career-advice/3-reasons-successful-professionals-hire-a-life-coach.

Wile, Douglas. *Lost T'ai-chi Classics from the Late Ch'ing Dynasty*. Albany: State University of New York Press, 1996.

Williamson, Marianne. *A Return to Love: Reflections on the Principles of "A Course in Miracles."* 2nd ed. New York: HarperCollins, 1996.

Wolinsky, Jacob. "Buffett and Munger: Staying Rational and Avoiding Confirmation Bias." ValueWalk. Accessed September 2009. https://www.valuewalk.com/2019/04/buffett-munger -rational-avoiding-confirmation-bias.

Zhu, Jessie. "What Is Self-Awareness and Why Is It Important? [+5 Ways to Increase It]." Positive Psychology. Accessed September 2019. https://positivepsychology.com/self-awareness -matters-how-you-can-be-more-self-aware.

Index

E

"Ego depletion," 3
Eisenhower's decision matrix, 72
Elton, Chester, 98
Emotions. *See also* Feelings
   negative, 34
   triggers and, 151
"Energetic determination," 5–6
Executive function, 5
Exercise, 52–53
Expectations, 38–39
"Extraneous Factors in Judicial
   Decisions," 145
Extrinsic motivators, 98

F

Failure, fear of, 68–69, 146
Feelings. *See also* Emotions
   of achievement, 41
   uncomfortable, 65–66
Feloni, Richard, 109
Fixed mindset, 10, 28–29
Flow, 79–80, 83
Focus, 138–139
Ford, Henry, 6
Fortune-telling, 67
Fresh starts, 116
Future self, 25–26, 31, 38–39

G

Glucose, 3, 145
Goals, 11–12, 18–19, 36, 107
Goleman, Daniel, 84
Gostick, Adrian, 98
Gratification, 108
Gratitude, 42
Growth mindset, 10–11, 28–29

H

Habits, 56–57, 68–69, 94
Humor, 117, 153

I

If-then statements, 32–33
Illeism, 54–55
Impulses, 123–124
Indulging, 105
Inner critic, 58–59
Inspiration, 134–135
Intention-setting, 32–33
Intrinsic motivators, 96–97, 100
James, LeBron, 55
Jordan, Michael, 39
Journaling, 71–72

L

Laughter therapy, 153
Lee, Kate, 45
Leroy, Sophie, 138
Light, 40

M

Magnification and
   minimization, 110–111
"Marshmallow experiment," 2, 47
Maslow's hierarchy of needs, 63
McGonigal, Kelly, 5, 27, 74, 95,
   105, 130–131
Meaning, finding, 48–49
Meditation, 125
Mental energy, 60
Mental filtering, 110–111
Mindfulness, 69, 125, 149–150
Mindset (Dweck), 28

Acknowledgments

To my editor, John: Thank you for your unwavering support and bearing with me through all my nitpicky edits—your understanding, positivity, and calm nature helped this first-time author out (more than you know!).

To my mother: I couldn't have written this book without you! Literally. Your wisdom and encouragement have meant everything to me. A sincere and whole-hearted thank you.

To my father: Same to you, Daddy-o. Thanks for believing in me, always.

To my husband, Mike: So appreciative of you—especially as our time together was more than cut in half during this process! And, while I know you've delighted in some newfound "you-time," I can't wait to finally spend some "us-time" together!

To my friends and colleagues: Lauren, Laura, Jamie, Melanie, Michelle, Lawren, Kelly, Emily, Abby, and the Zaza Gang, to name a few—your enthusiasm about this project has meant everything to me. I love you all.

To Carol Dweck, Brooke Castillo, Erik Barker, Kelly McGonigal, those at Boldheart and iPEC, the authors, teachers, and mentors, who've inspired me like crazy along the way: Thanks for your brilliance, leadership, passion, perseverance and, last but not least, your willpower. You've made a huge difference in my life.

To the reader: To you! You are my biggest source of inspiration. Thank you for reading, for taking a chance on this book, and more importantly, for taking a chance on you. If I can, you can. You already have what it takes.

And to my child due in June: Thanks for giving me ammo to do this not just for me, but for you, my sweet. Anything's possible!

About the Author

Aliya Levinson, LMSW, MA, CPC, ELI-MP, is a certified professional coach. She works with motivated men and women around the world to release self-doubt and indecision so they can finally embrace the peace, ease, and fulfillment that come with stepping into greater confidence and increased self-trust. She supports her clients in creating more freedom and meaning both personally and professionally by learning to live in alignment with their core values and develop, claim, and share their one-of-a-kind brilliance. Aliya also helps new and emerging life coaches successfully enroll clients and launch sustainable coaching practices.

In 2007, after the unexpected passing of her younger sister, Aliya realized the fragility of life and the importance of living life to the fullest. She made a promise to herself to shine her light brightly and create a thriving coaching practice that supports others. This book is part of that promise.

In addition to coaching, Aliya loves dancing, being with friends, discovering great restaurants in New York City, and spending time with her husband, Mike. To draft this book within 70 days while maintaining her full-time coaching practice and expecting their first child, Aliya relied on many of the willpower strategies detailed here. You can learn more at aliyalevinson.com.

CPSIA information can be obtained
at www.ICGtesting.com
Printed in the USA
LVHW051933220120
644449LV00026B/586

9 781646 113279